CHOOSING CHILDREN

Surely parents owe it to their children to give them the best life they can? Increasingly we are able to reduce the number of babies born with disabilities and disorders. But there is a powerful new challenge to conventional thinking about the desirability of doing so: it comes from those who actually have these conditions. They call into question the very definition of disability; how do we justify trying to avoid bringing people like them into being?

Jonathan Glover also examines the emotive idea of 'eugenics', and the ethics of attempting to enhance people genetically for non-medical reasons. Should parents be free to choose, for instance, the colour of their children's eyes or hair? This is no longer a distant prospect, but an existing power which we cannot wish away. What impact will such interventions have, both on the individuals concerned and on society as a whole? Is there a central core of human nature with which we must not interfere?

This beautifully clear book is written for anyone who cares about the rights and wrongs of parents' choices for their children, indeed for anyone concerned about the future of humanity.

Jonathan Glover is Professor of Ethics, and Director of the Centre for Medical Law and Ethics, at King's College London.

D1114325

UEHIRO SERIES IN PRACTICAL ETHICS

General editor: Julian Savulescu, University of Oxford

CHOOSING CHILDREN

Genes, Disability, and Design

Jonathan Glover

CLARENDON PRESS · OXFORD

OXFORD

UNIVERSITY PRESS

Great Clarendon Street, Oxford OX2 6DP

Oxford University Press is a department of the University of Oxford.
It furthers the University's objective of excellence in research, scholarship,
and education by publishing worldwide in

Oxford New York

Auckland Cape Town Dar es Salaam Hong Kong Karachi
Kuala Lumpur Madrid Melbourne Mexico City Nairobi
New Delhi Shanghai Taipei Toronto

With offices in

Argentina Austria Brazil Chile Czech Republic France Greece
Guatemala Hungary Italy Japan Poland Portugal Singapore
South Korea Switzerland Thailand Turkey Ukraine Vietnam

Oxford is a registered trade mark of Oxford University Press
in the UK and in certain other countries

Published in the United States
by Oxford University Press Inc., New York

First published 2006

First published in paperback 2007

British Library Cataloguing in Publication Data

Data available

Library of Congress Cataloging in Publication Data

Glover, Jonathan.
   Choosing children : genes, disability, and design / Jonathan Glover.
      p. cm.
   Includes bibliographical references and index.
   1. Genetic disorders in children.   2. Abnormalities, Human—Genetic
aspects.   3. Medical ethics.   4. Genetic counseling.   I. Title.
   RJ47.3.G556 2006   618.92′0042—dc22   2005030309

Typeset by Laserwords Private Limited, Chennai, India
Printed in Great Britain
on acid-free paper by
Clays Ltd., St Ives plc., Suffolk

3

ISBN 978–0–19–929092–5 (Hbk.)   978–0–19–923849–1 (Pbk.)

The Uehiro Series in Practical Ethics

In 2002 the Uehiro Foundation on Ethics and Education, chaired by Mr Eiji Uehiro, established the Uehiro Chair in Practical Ethics at the University of Oxford. The following year the Oxford Uehiro Centre for Practical Ethics was created within the Philosophy Faculty. Generous support by the Uehiro Foundation enabled the establishment of an annual lecture series, The Uehiro Lectures in Practical Ethics. These three lectures, given each year in Oxford, capture the ethos of the Oxford Uehiro Centre for Practical Ethics: to bring the best scholarship in analytic philosophy to bear on the most significant problems of our time. The aim is to make progress in the analysis and resolution of these issues to the highest academic standard in a manner that is accessible to the general public. Philosophy should not only create knowledge, it should make people's lives better. Each year's lectures are published by Oxford University Press as a book in the Uehiro Series in Practical Ethics. The inaugural Uehiro Lectures, attended by the Vice President of the Uehiro Foundation, Mr Tetsuji Uehiro, were given by Professor Jonathan Glover. They were entitled 'Choosing Children—Genes, Disability and Design.'

Julian Savulescu
Uehiro Chair in Practical Ethics
Director, Oxford Uehiro Centre for Practical Ethics
University of Oxford

Editor
The Uehiro Series in Practical Ethics

TO DAVID

Contents

Introduction

Progress in genetics and in reproductive technologies gives us growing power to reduce the incidence of disabilities and disorders. Should we welcome this power, or should we fear its implications?

The case for optimism is not hard to see. Disabilities and disorders often (though not always) mean that people have less good lives than they would have had. They may have lives with more pain and more periods in hospital than others have. They may find many things harder to achieve than others do. These disadvantages can be seen as a huge natural injustice, affecting many people, which wherever possible should be removed.

There is also the possibility of going beyond the reduction or elimination of disabilities and disorders. It may be possible for other genetic choices to give children a better start. Perhaps we will be able to give them a better chance of having abilities—or qualities of temperament and character—that will enrich their lives.

The case for pessimism is not hard to see either. The new science and medicine sometimes enable us to cure the disorders people have. But often, the elimination of disability is by means of preventing the birth of disabled people, whether by antenatal screening programmes or by pre-implantation genetic diagnosis. Some say this is like Nazi eugenics. There is also concern about the impact of these choices on people with disabilities already living in our society.

Some of the pessimism is linked to 'designer babies'. Perhaps some people would have better lives as a result of genes chosen for them. But who is to decide which changes are improvements? Here again, the state eugenic policies of the Nazis are a grim warning. Perhaps such choices should be left to parents. Ideas of parental procreative liberty are influential. But should there be limits to parents' genetic choices for their children? Perhaps children need protection from foolish or harmful choices. Do children have a right not to be designed by their parents at all? And might parental genetic choices have bad consequences for society as a whole? Remembering the sometimes harmful unintended consequences of technology, should we risk tampering with something so fundamental as people's genetic make-up?

This book is in three chapters. The first is about genetic choices linked to disability. Is it justifiable to use pre-implantation diagnosis with the aim of having a child who can hear or see rather than one who is deaf or blind? I will defend such choices against the charge of 'Nazi eugenics'. Is it right to choose a particular semen donor, as some have done, with the aim of having a child who *is* deaf? This raises the issue of what a disability is. I will give an account of disability that includes deafness, but will argue that choosing to have a deaf child can still in some circumstances be defended.

Any discussion of genetic choices aimed at having a child without disability has to take seriously the objection that such choices express attitudes that threaten the claim of disabled people to equality of respect. I will argue that this objection touches on something deep, yet is not decisive against these choices. But the best way of doing justice to the objection has some surprising implications. One is that the distinction between medical and non-medical genetic interventions may not have the moral importance many suppose.

The second chapter is about possible conflicts between parental freedom of choice and the interests of the child. Should parents be free to choose the genetic make-up of their children? Or do the interests of the child set limits to this? What do we owe to our children? I will argue that parental choice *should* be constrained by what we owe to our children. But often the right boundaries are not where conventional wisdom places them.

The last chapter is about genetic enhancement, or 'designer babies', where genes are chosen not on medical grounds but with the aim of giving other kinds of benefit. I will argue that crossing the boundary between medical intervention and enhancement is hard to rule out in principle. But genetic enhancement raises huge problems about its impact on society. There are problems about justice and about genetic competitiveness. Perhaps the deepest issue is whether there are parts of human nature that should be protected from the consequences of genetic choices. This is linked to the ancient philosophical question of what a good human life is.

Great changes in what human beings are like are becoming possible. We 'free-range' humans may have to decide for or against some of these changes. Some of the deepest philosophical questions hold the key to some of the most fundamental practical decisions the human race has ever had to make.

Chapter One
Disability and Genetic Choice

Since the 1980s, ethical debate about disabilities and disorders has been transformed by the participation of those who have these conditions. We now have a range of powerful descriptions of what it is like to be blind or deaf, and of the experience of having schizophrenia, manic depression, and other physical or psychiatric disorders. These contributions bring out sharply the limitations of previous discussions of a question like 'how serious a disadvantage is blindness/deafness/manic depression?' Without the input of first-person experience, these discussions are the intellectual equivalent of 'does he take sugar?' Of course, not all accounts from inside give the same message. (Some people do take sugar and some don't.) But, taken together, they have given the ethical discussions a human depth not found before.

People with these conditions have not only described them. They have also challenged previous thinking about disability. They have brought out the extent to which society's response to a medical condition contributes to whether or not it is a disability. They have forced the rest of us to confront some widespread and ugly attitudes towards people with disability. And, in the debates over the use of antenatal screening programmes or pre-implantation diagnosis to detect disabilities, some of them have raised the 'expressivist' objection. What attitudes towards disabled people do these programmes express, and what message do they send to

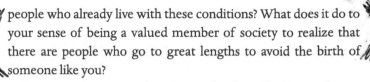

people who already live with these conditions? What does it do to your sense of being a valued member of society to realize that there are people who go to great lengths to avoid the birth of someone like you?

Some people use genetic and reproductive techniques to have a healthy child rather than one with a disability. Is this justifiable? There is also a 'reverse' version of this issue. Some people who are deaf have used pre-implantation diagnosis in order to have a deaf child rather than a hearing child.

In 2002 a lesbian couple, Sharon Duchesneau and Candy McCullough, who are both deaf, used sperm donated by a friend with hereditary deafness to have a deaf baby. They took the view that deafness is not a disability but a difference. During her pregnancy, Sharon Duchesneau said, 'It would be nice to have a deaf child who is the same as us ... A hearing baby would be a blessing. A deaf baby would be a special blessing.'[1]

The couple were criticized by some who take the view that deafness is a disability. Alta Charo, Professor of Law and Bioethics at the University of Wisconsin, asked whether they had 'violated the sacred duty of parenthood, which is to maximise to some reasonable degree the advantages available to their children'. She said: 'I'm loath to say it, but I think it's a shame to set limits on a child's potential.'[2]

Others came to the support of the couple. Sharon Ridgeway, who is the deaf mother of a deaf child, said: 'I in no way see deafness as a disability, but rather as a way into a very rich culture. Which is one of the reasons I was delighted to learn when I gave birth that my baby was deaf.'[3]

There is increasing support for the view that deafness is not a disability. The task force on cochlear implants of the (American) National Association of the Deaf said of some who advocate cochlear implants: 'They treat them as though they're hearing people who don't hear. It is like treating black people as white people with a skin disease.'

What counts as a disability and what is just a difference?

DISABILITY AND HUMAN FLOURISHING

Social and medical contributions to disability

Until the 1990s the conception of disability most people had was a purely medical one. Some physiological or chemical system might be missing or atrophied, or might have been damaged through illness, accident, or some other trauma. The absence or malfunctioning of such a system results in the person having impaired abilities to cope with life. A malfunctioning visual system causes the disability of blindness. A malfunctioning auditory system causes the disability of deafness. A stroke that disrupts systems involved in speech or movement causes corresponding disabilities.

Few would dispute that there is truth in this picture, but it is now clearer that it leaves out the enormous social contribution to disability. How far people who cannot walk have impaired abilities to cope with life depends on how many buildings, buses, and trains have wheelchair access, as well as on society's willingness to provide cars or wheelchairs to those who need but cannot afford them.[4]

The social contribution is not just a matter of the provision or absence of facilities. In the late nineteenth and early twentieth centuries, the disabling impact of deafness was greatly reduced for those who lived on Martha's Vineyard.[5] Because of hereditary deafness, one person there in every 155 was born deaf. This was more than thirty-five times the incidence in an average American community. The high, but apparently random, occurrence meant deafness was seen as something that could strike anyone. 'The deaf' were not a separate group.

Because there were so many deaf people, all using sign language, those with hearing also picked up sign and used it. A visiting reporter in 1895 described how spoken language and sign would 'be so mingled in the conversation that you pass from one to the other, or use both at once, almost unconsciously'.[6] This removed the usual communication barrier faced by deaf people. As a result, people hardly noticed who was deaf and who was not. Nora Ellen Groce interviewed old people who remembered those times. One said: 'It was taken pretty much for granted. It was as if somebody had brown eyes and somebody else had blue. Well, not quite so much—but as if, ah, somebody was lame and somebody had trouble with his wrist.' Another said: 'Oh, those people weren't handicapped. They were just deaf.'[7]

In the social impact on disability, people's reactions can be at least as important as wheelchair access or financial support. When the stigma of separateness and the communication barrier were both removed in Martha's Vineyard, deafness became insignificant as a disability. So it was not seen as a disability and this too made it less disabling.

There is some hope that stigma may also be reduced by greater understanding of genetics. We all carry several recessive mutations. This means that, as Julian Savulescu has put it, 'the clean white line between healthy and unhealthy will become grey smear'.[8]

There has been a debate over whether we should replace the 'medical' or 'functional' model of disability with the 'social-construction' model. It is time to give up this debate, as it is now unfruitful for the same reason that makes the 'nature–nurture' debate unfruitful. To many disabilities, there is a contribution from a variety of sources, including functional limitation *and* social context.[9] And social context may be very general (for instance, how much wheelchair access the society provides) or local (how does the person's family cope?).

These complex interactions have been recognized in the International Classification of Functioning, Disability, and Health (ICF), produced by the World Health Organization in 2001. They mention the medical and social models and produce their own 'biopsychosocial' approach, 'based on an integration of these two opposing models'.[10] The ICF classification distinguishes functional limitations (such as a heart condition), activity limitations (such as problems walking upstairs), and participation limitations (which may depend on whether lifts are provided or whether the meeting is moved downstairs).

This interactive model is clearly an advance. But there is still the problem raised by the question of whether deafness is a disability or just a difference. What counts as a functional limitation? Is the contrast with the average person or with some ideal? On what basis do we count a particular limitation as disabling? What should we say about functional limitations that do not impair activity or participation? Or about limitations of activity and participation that are purely social, without any functional limitation? What is the structure of the concept of disability?

What is disability?

All disabilities involve functional limitation. This contrasts with purely socially constructed disadvantages—for instance, those facing members of ethnic minorities in a racist society. We do not say someone's ethnicity is a disability, precisely because all its disadvantages are entirely socially imposed. In theory, social input is not in the same way essential for something to be a disability. Robinson Crusoe, alone on his island and unable to walk properly after a stroke, would still be disabled. (Of course in practice most disability has a social input.)

Disability requires failure or limitation of functioning. But a limitation of functioning creates disability only if (on its own or *via* social discrimination) it impairs capacities for human flourishing. It would not be a disability if there were a failure of a system whose only function was to keep toenails growing. With arrested toenail growth, we flourish no less.

Why 'impaired *capacities* for human flourishing' rather than just 'impaired human flourishing'? Colour blindness is a disability that excludes someone from becoming a pilot. But suppose someone colour-blind does not want to become a pilot or do any of the other things that depend on normal colour vision. The incapacity does not reduce the person's flourishing. The choice is between saying that for him or her it is a harmless disability or saying it is not a disability at all. There is a verbal choice here, and in this case it does not greatly matter which way we go. The choice becomes more important where what people want to do is shaped by their reduced capacities.

On this account, disability involves a functional limitation, which (either on its own or—more usually—in combination with social disadvantage) impairs the capacity for human flourishing.

One implication of this is to raise doubts about the boundary between what is conventionally thought of as disability and what is conventionally classified as medical disorder. A heart condition that stops someone doing football or athletics, or diabetes with its restricted diet, or schizophrenia, are all conventionally seen as disorders rather than disabilities. But they all involve functional limitations that, to very different degrees, impair human flourishing. Perhaps the more serious chronic medical disorders that restrict what people do should all be thought of as disabilities.[11]

This account excludes from disability conditions whose disadvantage is purely social. Belonging to a minority that suffers discrimination is not a disability. One consequence may be the need to reclassify some conditions now thought of as disabilities. For instance, achondroplasia, severely restricted height resulting from a genetic mutation, is normally classified as a disability. But the purely functional impairments are trivial, such as needing a stool to boost height when speaking in public. Provided that there are no associated medical complications, the only serious disadvantages result from the reactions of other people. This makes it the same as being Jewish in an anti-Semitic society or gay in a homophobic society. This could push us towards saying that sometimes ethnic or religious membership, or sexual orientation, can count as a disability. Or, with less offence to our linguistic and moral intuitions, we can say that achondroplasia is not a disability.

To link disability with impaired capacities for human flourishing is plausible, even platitudinous. But there are problems about what counts as human flourishing and about how we identify impaired capacities for it. There are some severe cases of disability where the issues are relatively uncontroversial. But in less extreme cases the impact on human flourishing is not so obvious.

The contrast with normal human functioning

Nearly all of us who have no recognized disability, perhaps *all* of us, still have functional limitations compared to the average person. We may be below average in colour vision or in musical ear, or we may have below average muscular coordination. Again, it is a continuum of severity, and the boundary between normality and disability is often a blurred one.

In another way we all have functional limitations. All of us lack the capacity for unaided detection of radio waves or X-rays. We all lack wings that would enable us to fly. We do not say that everyone is disabled because of lacking these abilities. We count functional limitations as disabilities only when there is a contrast with normal human functioning.

This account of disability is in agreement with the idea of a 'natural defect' developed by Philippa Foot and Michael Thompson. Lameness, blindness, and colour blindness are seen to be natural defects by comparison with functioning that is normal for the species.[12] Philippa Foot suggests that this 'functioning' contributes to the good of the individual species member. She interprets this as survival and reproduction in the case of non-human species, but says that the list of human goods is not exhausted by survival and reproduction. Among the things needed for a good human life are the physical and mental capacities for learning language and the powers of imagination to understand stories, to join in songs and dances, and to laugh at jokes.[13]

Philippa Foot says the good for all other species is exhausted by survival and reproduction, while for humans it includes such things as participating in songs and dances. One question is whether this is too limited a view of the good for members of some other species. It may underrate the kinds of emotion, communication, and play that are open, for instance, to dolphins. If our songs and dances enable our good to transcend mere survival and reproduction, it seems arbitrary to reject what dolphins do with whistling as grounds for the same transcendence.[14]

In the case of human beings, there are questions about the boundaries of the normality that is contrasted with disability.

What is normal human functioning?

Various possible changes in human functioning raise doubts about whether normality here is a purely statistical concept. Suppose HIV/AIDS spread so much that most people in the world were affected by it. We would surely continue to see the impaired capacities caused by the disease as disabilities, despite their numerical predominance. We appeal to a 'normative norm' as well as a statistical one. The contrast here would be with people in the pre-AIDS past, whose unimpaired functioning provided the relevant standard.

But, in the case of enhancements in functioning, ideas of normality might change. If a widespread mutation (or widespread use of genetic engineering) gave most people wings, those of us still unable to fly might start to count as disabled. But, with very rare enhancements, the benchmark would be less likely to change. If we discovered an intellectual enhancement that so far had been possessed only by Newton and Einstein, the rest of us would probably not come to see ourselves as cognitively disabled.

The normality that is contrasted with disability is a hybrid of the numerical and the normative. Its possession by a reasonable sized group is needed if something is to count as normal functioning. But numbers can sometimes be overridden by a higher level of functioning, either by a current one that supersedes the past norm, or by a past statistical norm that puts present reality in the shade. The central idea seems to be that of a benchmark of human potentiality, demonstrated by some sizeable past or present population.

At the margins, a conception of normal human functioning may also reflect social attitudes.[15] We include different sexual orientations within normal species functioning, while those who in the 1950s treated being gay as 'un-natural' took a different view.

The relevant concept of normality is a messy one. It is partly socially constructed. It is partly context dependent. And it combines elements of the numerical and the normative.

This messiness gives appeal to the idea of looking for a simpler and clearer concept of disability. John Harris points out that numerical predominance of a characteristic is compatible with its being a disability. He says: 'Normal species functioning cannot form part of the definition of disability because people might be normal and still disabled.' He proposes an alternative account: disability is 'a condition that someone has a strong rational preference not to be in'. It is 'a harmful condition' relative, not to normal functioning, but to possible alternatives. To illustrate his conception of harm, he uses the idea of a condition—for instance, a little finger severed at the first joint—such that hospital staff would be negligent if they did not bother to attempt to repair it in an unconscious patient.[16]

This account of disability avoids the messy complexities of the contrast with normal functioning. But it seems to cast the net too wide. Suppose people are ranked along some dimension, perhaps intelligence, sporting skills, attractiveness, or cheerfulness. A particular person just a little below average could perfectly rationally have a strong preference to be further up the scale. This might enhance his or her career, love life, or happiness. But it seems sweeping to say that anyone dissatisfied with his or her ranking counts as disabled. The rational reconstruction is at the cost of great detachment from the ordinary concept of disability. To stay within the everyday sense of the word, I will stick to the admittedly messy contrast with normal functioning.

Moral objections to the contrast with normality

Sometimes the contrast between potentially disabling functional limitations and normal human functioning is seen as morally objectionable. Anita Silvers has argued that the emphasis on normality may be used to support coercion of people with anomalous functioning, as when deaf people were forced to use 'normal' oral language rather than sign.[17] That coercion was indeed harsh and unjustifiable.

And it may be that an emphasis on trying to recover normality contributed to the coercion. Clare Sainsbury, writing of her experience of Asperger's syndrome, says that 'normal' people take it as a basic human right to be accepted as they are, while 'the rest of us are viewed only in terms of what will make us more acceptable to them'. She adds that 'the philosophy of normalization seems painfully familiar to those of us whose very disability lies in our "differentness". Most of us have spent years being taught that who we are is fundamentally wrong and in need of cure.'[18]

Clare Sainsbury is right to condemn that version of 'the philosophy of normalization'. But an account of disability that contrasts it with normal functioning need not support this Procrustean approach. Such an account marks off some barriers to human flourishing as potential disabilities by means of the contrast with normal human functioning. This need not create some fetish about everyone being the same. Mere normality or abnormality is unimportant. What matters is the contribution to whether or not the person flourishes. And, unsurprisingly, people with Asperger's syndrome flourish more when not forced into attempts to conform, and deaf people flourish more when they choose for themselves whether to use sign.

Impaired human flourishing: the case of blindness

Aristotle was a biologist as well as a philosopher. When he made the idea of human flourishing the centre of his ethical theory, he may have been thinking of humans as one species among others.

When we look at other species, we often have quite strong intuitive ideas about what constitutes (and especially what does *not* constitute) flourishing for them. To cage birds seems an outrage because such a life denies their nature. A bird does not flourish unless it is able to use its wings and fly. One thought is that human nature in the same way may determine the contours of the good life for us.

There is no one recipe for human flourishing. It takes all sorts to make a world. Wrestlers may flourish in one way, nurses in another. The good life for a Russian peasant may not be the good life for a Hollywood actor. Teenage boys may flourish differently from grandmothers.

Even so, there may be some shared human values, so that we can have a rough idea of some likely ingredients of a good life, to be variously combined in different people's recipes and in their lives. Again, the point is made more easily in terms of what does *not* count as a good life. Many would agree that people's lives are likely to be made worse by having their children forcibly removed, or by long periods of excruciating pain, or by mindless soul-destroying work or enforced solitary confinement.

There are exceptions. A masochist has reason to accept some pain. Someone with a particular religious vocation may choose to accept imposed solitary confinement in a nunnery or a monastery. These are cases where the badness is instrumental to recognizable human goods such as sexual or religious fulfilment. The extent to which particular dimensions of the good life would command universal or near-universal agreement is a complex empirical question. Do the senses of hearing and sight count as dimensions of human flourishing, such that deprivation of them is a disability?

Some reflection on these questions has been by those with experience of functional impairment. The philosopher Martin

Milligan, who was blind from a very early age, thought that some sighted people greatly exaggerate the importance of seeing. He thought that, because sighted people use sight so much, they underrate the information other senses give and also the information communicated by language. But he also thought of blindness as 'a major handicap and deprivation'. Blind people are not cut off from the world, but they lack the perception of detail that enables safe navigation through it. He knew that others thought of it as a difference rather than a disability, but he argued that it is 'a "difference" which is so disadvantaging in such a wide range of frequently encountered circumstances that those who suffer from it should ... be counted as suffering from a serious *general* handicap'.[19]

Here we can draw on our other resource: the knowledge all those with a particular sense have of how much it does or does not contribute to our lives. As Martin Milligan recognized, the contribution of sight to human flourishing goes beyond safe navigation through the world. Perhaps those of us who are sighted exaggerate the functional importance of vision. But it is hard to exaggerate the way our lives are enriched by the light and the sky at different times of day and at different seasons, by the light in a painting by Vermeer, by the visual excitement of New York, or by the combination of the colour and architectural completeness of Siena. (Or by the sight of either Radcliffe Square or New College cloisters at night.) It is almost impossible to exaggerate the enrichment that comes from seeing other people, their bodies, and especially their faces. (And, possibly most of all, by what eye contact contributes to relationships.)

Our love of seeing things may go back as far as the human race does. It certainly goes back as far as the pre-Socratic philosophers. Anaxagoras, when asked why it was worth being born rather than not, replied: 'for the sake of viewing the heavens and the whole order of the universe.'[20] Since sight enriches our lives so much, it is hard not to see blindness as an obstacle to flourishing.

The evidence of preferences

In thinking about whether a condition impairs human flourishing, we can often draw on accounts by people with experience of it. If *they* do not think it impairs their flourishing, this should have an impact on how the rest of us see it.

On an Australian television programme, there was a discussion between a geneticist and Dr Tom Shakespeare, a sociologist widely known for academic work that brings ethics into contact with the experience of disability. Dr Shakespeare also has achondroplasia. The geneticist said he was sure that 'Dr Shakespeare would prefer not to be handicapped'. Dr Shakespeare replied: 'I'm happy the way I am. I would never have wanted to be different.'[21] This gives some support to the view that achondroplasia is not a disability, but a difference.

But the preferences may need interpretation. There are different possible reasons for the willing acceptance of a functional limitation generally seen as disabling. One is that disabilities can have their compensations. In some cases these are 'external'. A dramatic case was the welcome given in the First World War to the wounds that meant repatriation from the trenches. Another case is where deafness may be a passport to acceptance in the deaf community.

Compensations may be internal to the condition itself. Manic depression severely limits a person's functioning and is horrible to experience. But sometimes those who have it, at least when it is controlled by medication, find the terrible aspects outweighed by the heightened emotional intensity it brings.[22] For the person's potential to flourish, it is still in some respects devastating. This is

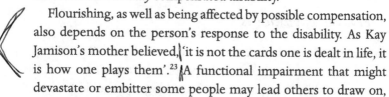

why it counts as a disorder or disability. But, for some people, the enhancements it brings make it a disability they do not regret. For them it is an *internally* compensated disability.

Flourishing, as well as being affected by possible compensation, also depends on the person's response to the disability. As Kay Jamison's mother believed, 'it is not the cards one is dealt in life, it is how one plays them'.[23] A functional impairment that might devastate or embitter some people may lead others to draw on, and be enriched by, qualities of character they hardly knew they had. (The dangers of pushing this line of thought too far, of being complacent about 'ennobling' disadvantage, are obvious.)

Disadvantage can itself shape people's preferences. Jon Elster, using the Aesopian phrase 'sour grapes', has raised questions about these 'adaptive preferences'. He suggests that 'we should not take wants as given, but inquire into their rationality or autonomy'.[24] In development economics, Amartya Sen has made a powerful case for not taking the satisfaction of scaled-down preferences as enough to show that people are flourishing.[25] In India, China, and other countries, women on average have less access to education or medical care than men do. Many women there hold beliefs that make them willingly accept all this as right and proper. But this does not end all doubts about how far they are flourishing. Getting what you want is not all there is to a good life. A lot depends on whether your preferences and hopes are themselves impoverished.

John Stuart Mill's sometimes derided discussion of 'higher and lower pleasures' is relevant here.[26] Unlike Bentham, he wanted a version of utilitarianism where poetry ranked higher than pushpin. His idea of assessing people's happiness included an estimate of the *quality* of their pleasures. What made one pleasure of higher quality than another was that it would be preferred when choices were made by 'competent judges' who had experience of both states. As a test for quality of pleasure, this test is only intermittently effective, something known to all those of us who sometimes watch a television game show when we could be reading Proust.

But, as one test of whether a functional impairment restricts flourishing, it is obviously worth listening to what is said by people who have known life without it and life with it.

Many people have made the transition to having a disability. John Hull has given a powerful description of the disorientation and sense of loss he felt after going blind. At first the problems of blindness posed challenges to overcome. Then there was a period of despair: 'the horror of the receding light, of the experience of going deeper and deeper down, of the revulsion and rejection one feels in the presence of an irretrievable loss and at the sense of being trapped in there forever.'[27]

At that stage he had terrible dreams. In one he was on a waterlogged ocean liner sinking beneath the sea, while the ship he had been on before sailed away. In another dream he was in a truck in a mineshaft going into the side of a mountain. The light was still visible behind, but grew smaller as the truck went deeper into the rock.

So much was taken away that a huge personal reconstruction was needed.

Blindness is like a huge vacuum cleaner which comes down upon your life, sucking almost everything away. Your past memories, your interests, your perception of time and how you will spend it, place itself, even the world, everything is sucked out. Your consciousness is evacuated, and you are left to reconstruct it, including a new sense of time, a new realization of the body in space and so on.[28]

Later came a turning point. 'Going back to the image of the tunnel, I have turned a corner. The pinpoint of light seems to have vanished.'[29] Acceptance went with the growth of inner resources.

As one goes deeper and deeper into blindness the things which were once taken for granted, and which were then mourned over as they disappeared, and for which one tried in various ways to find compensation, in the end cease to matter. Somehow it no longer seems important what people look like, or what cities look like ... One begins to live by other interests, other values. One begins to take up residence in another world.[30]

A few people have started in that 'other world' and have made the transition the other way, to being sighted. John Hull found the vacuum of blindness sucked away so much that he had to reconstruct his conception, not only of the world but also of himself and his past. Those moving from blindness to sight may have faced similar challenges. Often the operation that gives sight is followed by a psychological crisis.

Richard Gregory and Jean G. Wallace have described what happened to 'S.B.' when he was given sight by an operation.[31] He had been blind since he was a few months old. As a blind man, he was cheerful, confident, and dominating. He took pride in his skills as a carpenter and cobbler. When in hospital after the operation, he took pleasure in recognizing cars and other objects and in drawing houses and buses. He was proud of being able to write a version of his name. But when he left hospital things went downhill. He was unresponsive to his first drive (to London), complaining that the world seemed a drab place. He found the buildings of London dull and (for the first time) was frightened by traffic. He seemed to have lost interest in his surroundings.

He never again recovered his confidence and cheerfulness. Six months after the operation he was depressed. He seemed to have moved from being a blind man who coped well to being a man who used vision but coped poorly with it. Gregory and Wallace wrote that his previous achievements seemed paltry and his present position almost foolish. Later, his wife wrote that he was unwell ('His nerves are so bad') and that he was 'very disappointed about everything'. Twenty-one months after the operation he died. Gregory and Wallace wrote that when blind he had lived with energy and enthusiasm, but when given sight he lost his peace and self-respect.[32]

Not everyone who has made the transition has a psychological crisis. Mike May was totally blind from 3 until 46, when surgery gave him a moderate degree of sight. He is severely short-sighted. He takes a cheerful view of the operation. He says his coping techniques are '90% from the perspective of a totally blind person and 10% that of a visually impaired person' and that 'I am currently blessed to have the benefits of both worlds'. He read about the psychological crisis of S.B. only after his own surgery. He puts the happier outcome in his own case down to the richness of his own life as a blind person. He did not then have the sense of being limited and he had no expectation of sight being a huge enrichment of life. 'I expected new and interesting experiences from getting vision as an adult but not that it would change my life. So whereas others have slipped into depression from their experiences, I am enjoying my new visual tools and the fascinating entertainment it affords me.'[33]

What do these different responses to the transition, in one direction or the other, say about the impact of blindness or sight and human flourishing?

John Hull's powerful account of his sense of being trapped and of 'irretrievable loss' seems to support the view of blindness as a severe impairment of human flourishing. His preference is clear. But reports of S.B. and others who have had psychological crises after becoming sighted suggest that their preference was the other way. None of them, to my knowledge, has given a first-person account. But it is not hard to guess some causes of their preference for their previous state. Perhaps they had too high expectations. There are the problems of acquiring so many new skills, and the loss of self-respect that went with their difficulties. But there are also issues about the upheaval of their identity.

On going blind, John Hull faced the daunting difficulties of reconstructing his whole conception of the world and of himself. Something similar must have faced S.B. Even Mike May, reflecting on his successful transition, says that, 'in the newly sighted, learning to see demands a radical change in neurological functioning and, with it, a radical change in psychological functioning, in self, in identity . . . One must die as a blind person to be born again as a seeing person.'[34]

The question these comparisons raise is how far the disaster of going blind is because blindness in itself impairs flourishing. How big is the contribution of the transition problems, the huge upheaval in conceptions of the self and the world? In different cases, the preferences go different ways. In something so deep, how far are our preferences shaped by the blind or sighted world we have inhabited, and by the identity resulting from it? Because of these questions, we cannot just read off conclusions about the relative flourishing of blind and sighted people from uninterpreted preferences.

This is not an argument for discarding first-person accounts and the preferences they reveal. We do not want to return to 'does he take sugar?' evaluations purely from the outside. John Stuart Mill was not wrong about the relevance of those opinions. But they need to be interpreted with alertness to possible biases. And we need to combine them with our other sources of evidence. We can draw on the knowledge every hearing and sighted person has of the contribution these senses make to our lives, as well as on the history of reflection on the components of human flourishing. In that context, carefully interpreted first-person accounts are important evidence.

Choosing deafness and the interests of the child

I have argued that blindness impairs human flourishing. Parallel things can be said about deafness. The deaf child will not hear the car coming. Like blindness, deafness impairs safe navigation through the world. But there is also the loss of a whole dimension of enriching experience: the sounds of rivers and waterfalls, of male and female voices, of laughter, of tractors and birds, of coffee bubbling, of the baby's first cry, of the whole of music. It is hard not to see deafness too as an obstacle to human flourishing.

What implications does this have for the decision to aim for a deaf rather than a hearing child? Go back to Gauvin, the son of Sharon Duchesneau and Candy McCullough. If the line of thought here is right, deafness is not just a difference. But the couple can still be defended against the criticism that they have violated a sacred duty of parenthood. Their son, Gauvin, has not been harmed by what they did. If they had not sought out a donor with hereditary deafness, they might have had another child who was not deaf. But Gauvin himself would not have existed.

There are subtle issues (raised by 'wrongful-life' cases) about whether the idea of harm or benefit can ever apply to bringing someone into existence. But, if it does make sense to say that someone has been harmed by being brought into existence, this can be true only in cases where the person has reason to regret being alive, where life is so bad as to be 'not worth living'. It is obviously absurd to say this simply because someone is deaf. As Alta Charo rightly says, 'all of us recognize that deaf children can have perfectly wonderful lives'.[35] Gauvin's birth is not a disaster for him just because some other child who might have been born instead would have been able to hear.

Since genetic and reproductive technologies widened the range of choices about having children, one of the most often misused arguments has been 'it is not fair on the child'. When older women or lesbian couples have used techniques of assisted reproduction to have children, objectors have said that the interests of the child must be paramount. But the child is harmed only if the supposed disadvantages of being brought up by an older woman, or being brought up by two female parents, mean that it would be better for the child not to have been born.

People can be misled here by the model of adoption. Suppose that it is better to have a younger mother. Those trying to find an adoptive family for a child should think of the child's interests. Then, other things equal, perhaps they should opt for a younger rather than an older mother. But, where an older woman wants help to have a child, it is not a choice between her and some other woman as mother of the child. The choice is between the child being her child or not existing at all. Some of us are sceptical about the degree of the disadvantage of having an older mother, and about there being any disadvantage at all in having lesbian parents. But any disadvantage that does exist can hardly be great enough to make life not worth living. In these cases, the 'harm-to-the-child' objection has no force at all.

The same applies to the objection that choosing a deaf child violates a sacred duty of parenthood. If deafness is a disability, Gauvin has a disadvantage compared to a hearing child his parents might have had. Each of us has some disadvantage or other compared to some different child our parents might have had instead. But this does not mean that, in having us, our parents harmed us.

Against this, John Harris has argued that, when parents bring a deaf child into the world, when they could have had a hearing child, they do harm the child they have. He says they do not *wrong* the child. Since for that child the alternative was non-existence, he or she has no complaint. But they do harm the child: 'a harmed condition obtains whenever someone is in a disabling or hurtful condition, even though that condition is only marginally disabling and even though it is not possible for that particular individual to avoid the condition in question.'[36]

Rebecca Bennett, in her debate with John Harris on this issue, has argued that the parents do not harm the child, who 'has not been denied anything he could have ever possibly had'.[37] Harris and Bennett are using two different conceptions of harm. Bennett's seems closer to the ordinary conception. For Harris, anyone in any disadvantageous condition is harmed by whoever caused him or her to be in that condition. Because all of us have some disadvantages, we have all been harmed by the parents who caused our birth. To Harris, Philip Larkin's gloomy conception of the role of 'your Mum and Dad' must seem a huge understatement, as Larkin thought they started to 'fuck you up' only after birth. I salute John Harris's cheerful espousal of the even gloomier view, but will not follow him.

So the deaf child has not been harmed by being brought into the world. But there is a potential complication. Suppose the parents, having chosen an appropriate donor, have the deaf child they want. The child is glad to be alive, but deafness still restricts flourishing. If a cochlear implant is possible, should the parents choose it for the child?

When cochlear implants work, they enable people previously deaf to hear. Some people who remember having natural hearing say that, after an implant, the sounds at first are tinny by comparison. But their awareness of this fades. Some children who have cochlear implants are enthusiastic, as are their parents. But results vary according to individual circumstances. Where children in a deaf community already communicate by means of both sign and writing, the diversion of time from using sign to speech and hearing training can hold back their development.[38]

Cochlear implants are controversial, not just because their success is patchy, or because there may be a conflict between learning to hear and the use of sign. Some who see deafness as a difference rather than a disability see cochlear implants as an example of the objectionable imposition of 'normality', like treating black people as white people with a skin disease. And those of us who do see deafness as a disability do not have to think that 'normalizing' is the best strategy for helping deaf people flourish.

As things are now, a parental decision about whether or not a child should have an implant must often be very difficult. There is probably no one answer that is right for every family.

But, as a thought experiment, imagine these problems are overcome. Suppose we reach a stage where the implants work without complications, and ways are found of making children comfortably bilingual in sign and speech. What then should the parents do for the deaf child they have chosen? They did not harm the child by their choice of deaf donors. But perhaps, when the perfect version of the cochlear implant is available, parents will harm a child they leave deaf. The view that deafness is a disability supports the view that parents who can give their child hearing should do so. If that is accepted, the choice of a deaf child becomes self-defeating.

EUGENICS?

Look now at a far more common form of choice. People use antenatal screening or pre-implantation genetic diagnosis to have a child without a disability. Is this a form of eugenics? Is it part of a slide towards what the Nazis did?

Genetic choices and Nazi eugenics

In the first half of the twentieth century, eugenic ideas were popular, not only in Germany but also in the United States, Britain, Sweden, and other countries. People were worried that the average IQ might fall if less intelligent families had more children. They were worried that modern medicine frustrated the Darwinian process of selection. By enabling people with genetic disorders to live long enough to have children, was it increasing the incidence of those disorders? These worries led to support for the idea of eugenic policies: encouraging some people to have no children and others to have more children according to the likely impact on the gene pool.

The Nazis combined these ideas with a social Darwinist ideology that saw human life as a constant struggle for survival between different races or nations. A 'better' gene pool would give a nation a competitive advantage in the struggle. So Germans of the right kind (the blonde, athletic 'Aryan' type: roughly, people who did not look like Hitler) were encouraged through the Lebensborn programme to breed together. And people of the wrong kind (for instance, people with psychiatric illnesses) were to be discouraged from breeding, if necessary by forcible sterilization. Feelings of compassion for individuals were a form of weakness, when the struggle demanded hardness. Individuals did not matter. The survival of the race did. The toughness went further. Seventy thousand people in psychiatric hospitals were murdered by gassing. Some who started with these murders went on to take part in the Nazi genocide.

After this history, the standing of eugenics is deservedly not what it was in 1930. Few now warm to plans for improving the gene pool. Some worry that antenatal screening programmes and pre-implantation genetic diagnosis may be a stealthy return of eugenics. These techniques allow decisions about who will live to be made once again on the basis of genetic characteristics.

The concern depends partly on the ambiguity of the word 'eugenics'. Understood narrowly, it refers to social policies aimed at improving the gene pool. Understood broadly, it refers to any decision, including parental decisions, about what sort of child will be born. Objections to the narrow version cannot simply be assumed without argument to carry over to the other version.

It is worth pointing out that the values of the Nazis were utterly different from the values guiding parents who want their child not to have a disability.

Sometimes parents have already had one child with a severe genetic disorder. If the child had a short and painful life, the parents may not want to impose such a life on another child. Or the earlier child may still be alive, and the parents may feel unable to cope with two children with the disorder. Or, parents planning their first child may choose if possible to have a child without the problems caused by even a relatively mild disorder. The screening programme may be offered in the spirit of respecting their choice.

The values guiding all this could hardly be more different from those of the Nazis. There is no mention of the race or the gene pool. Instead of the subordination of the individual to the social Darwinist struggle for survival, there is compassion for the potential child. Instead of coercion by the state, there is respect for parental choice. And, perhaps most important of all, these parental choices are compatible with an attitude of equality of respect for everyone. Choosing to have a child without certain disabilities need not come from any idea that disabled people are inferior. Nor does it entail that the world, or the gene pool, should be cleansed of disabled people.

So the first thing to say about the comparison with Nazi eugenics is that those who make it usually do so at some distance from any serious knowledge of what the Nazis did.

Some ugly attitudes towards people with disabilities and disorders

It is nevertheless worth discussing one residual worry about attitudes underlying modern screening programmes and the use of pre-implantation genetic diagnosis. I mentioned that parental choice to have a child without certain disabilities need not be linked to any lack of respect for people with disabilities. But could it be that sometimes such choices do in fact reflect such attitudes?

There was a time when people, in other respects humane and highly civilized, could display some chilling attitudes. In 1915 Virginia Woolf in her diary described an encounter when walking by the Thames near Richmond.

On the towpath we met & had to pass a long line of imbeciles. The first was a very tall young man, just queer enough to look twice at, but no more; the second shuffled, & looked aside; & then one realised that everyone in that long line was a miserable ineffective shuffling idiotic creature, with no forehead, or no chin, & an imbecile grin, or a wild suspicious stare. It was perfectly horrible. They should certainly be killed.[39]

That such sentiments are today impossible to express (and, one hopes, to have) is one result of their being taken quite literally and acted upon by the Nazis. But their stark expression in 1915 raises the question of whether some milder version lingers on today.

Because they are included in current debates on these issues, people who themselves have disabilities and disorders draw attention to some ugly attitudes they have encountered. There has been the history of imposing 'normality', of stopping deaf people using sign, of not respecting the differences of people with Asperger's syndrome. Martin Milligan wrote about job discrimination against blind people. He was told he could not have a job because there were stairs. Blind people manage stairs perfectly well.

It is common to assume that people with disabilities must have a severely reduced quality of life, or even that their lives are likely to be barely worth living. Jane Campbell chairs the Social Care Institute for Excellence and is a disability-rights commissioner. She also has spinal muscular atrophy. She was in hospital with severe pneumonia.

On two separate occasions, doctors told me they assumed that if I fell unconscious I wouldn't want to be given life-saving treatment. I was so frightened of what might happen to me that I kept myself awake for 48 hours. My husband brought in a photo of me in my graduation gown and stuck it on the bed-head to remind the hospital staff that there was more to me than the shrivelled form they saw lying in front of them. I was lucky: although I could barely breathe, I had an assertive husband insisting to the authorities that I had everything to live for. Imagine what it would be like if you were too weak to communicate. Or your relatives less positive about the quality of your life.[40]

There is the tendency to think of a disability as a person's main feature. Sheila Hale describes a doctor telling her that giving her husband rehabilitation after his stroke would be futile:

It would be a waste of limited resources. He suggested I put John in a home. After all, he said, You're still relatively young. You don't want to spend the rest of your life tied to an infarct. I've looked up this word. It means a region of dead tissue caused by a blocked artery.[41]

Then there is the tendency to shy away from people with disability. Michael Mason, after having a stroke, noticed how being in a wheelchair made people sometimes talk to him through others. But then, with characteristic honesty, he remembered this kind of response, which so many of us fall into, from the inside. He wrote:

'Does he take sugar?' is a phrase which brilliantly captures this sense of being out of the human loop. It is one of many shaming memories about how I used to behave and feel in relation to the 'disabled' that I knew the man who coined this phrase (one of the last people to contract polio in this country) and yet always felt squeamish in his company. What exactly was going on down by his pelvis? Brrr... one didn't want to think. I would try and avoid physical meetings with him, vaguely ashamed of my physical distaste, but still preferring to sweep the whole thing under the carpet.[42]

Others have speculated about this shying away. David Wright has described how, when he first tells someone he is deaf, for a moment the person is embarrassed:

Though why he should be is never clear. There may be a built-in animal reaction that makes us resent, just a little, disability in another. Wolves turn upon a wounded member of the pack. *Homo sapiens* does not go that far, but the subconscious response, however minimal, however overlaid with inhibitions and social or ethical training, however instantly disguised as pity, is of the same order.[43]

These ugly attitudes sometimes appear when a possible child may have a disability or disorder. There can be pressures to terminate a pregnancy. One pregnant woman was offered a test for Down syndrome, which she refused because she would not want to terminate the pregnancy. She describes the midwife being outraged: 'It was irresponsible for someone "so old" to take "such a high risk" of having a Down's Syndrome child. I was made to feel dreadful.' After her pregnancy miscarried, she adopted a daughter. As her daughter has disabilities, she meets other parents whose children have disabilities: 'There is a great deal of self-generated guilt in these people at having "given their children problems" but then there is the other guilt that "outsiders" generate when they ask, quite openly and without embarrassment, "couldn't you have found out and had an abortion?" '[44]

The pressure not to have children with disabilities extends to children with psychiatric disorders. Kay Redfield Jamison, a distinguished psychologist who has co-authored the major textbook on manic depression, and who also has the illness, describes a physician asking about her psychiatric history and then asking if she planned to have children. When she said she wanted children, he asked her if she knew manic-depressive illness was a genetic disease. Stifling an urge to remind him about her professional life, she said she did. He said: 'You shouldn't have children. You have manic-depressive illness.' With a sarcasm he seemed not to notice, Kay Jamison asked whether this was because she would be an inadequate mother or because it was best not to bring another manic-depressive into the world. He replied, 'Both'. Kay Jamison describes how distressing she found these brutal comments. Her own response goes to the heart of the issue, saying that 'it had never occurred to me not to have children simply because I had manic-depressive illness. Even in my blackest depressions, I never regretted having been born... I was enormously glad to have been born, grateful for life, and I couldn't imagine not wanting to pass on life to someone else.'[45]

Equality of respect

In October 2003 some parents of children with Down syndrome wrote to a newspaper about the guidance on offering tests for Down syndrome, which had been newly issued by the National Institute for Clinical Excellence. The parents complained that, while the guidance recommended giving accurate information about the tests, it made no such recommendation about information about the syndrome itself. These parents suggested that lack of knowledge and lack of respect for people with Down syndrome led to unnecessary abortions. They asked:

Does British society really want to make this statement to our children with the syndrome, and the many adults with it who are living independent, fulfilling and wonderful lives, that they shouldn't be here; they are such a burden that they should be eradicated before birth?[46]

The letter from these parents was followed by a letter from a 12 year old, the older sister of a girl with Down syndrome. She asked: 'Please tell us what to say to Alice to explain that she is no use to society and that the society she lives in wishes she had been killed.'[47]

This line of thought, often called the 'expressivist' argument, is very powerful. Given the existence of some ugly attitudes towards disabled people, it is a reasonable worry that genetic choices against disability may express some of these attitudes. What does it do for a disabled person's sense of having equality of respect with other members of society if there are programmes designed to prevent the birth of people with his or her disability?

But, on the other hand, is it wrong to aim to have children who will flourish as much as possible? Is it right to have less flourishing children in order to avoid sending an undesirable signal to other people?

The decision not to have a child with a disability may be an expression of ugly attitudes towards people with disability. But equally it may not.

Mary Ann Baily, in the context of explaining her own decision to have amniocentesis, has made the point that choices against disability need not express the ugly attitudes. She explicitly rejects

33

the belief that people with disabilities cannot have fulfilling lives, and knows that parenting a disabled child can be rewarding. She opposes pressuring women into abortion on grounds of disability and supports more resources being used to help people with disabilities. Her decision expressed none of the ugly attitudes: 'It expresses only the fact that, given a choice, I would rather my child did not have a disability.'[48]

People sometimes choose to delay having children until they have more money and can afford to spend more on giving them a better start in life. This does not express contempt for poorer children. It merely expresses a desire to have children who have a better chance of having more flourishing lives. Because money is not everything, the plan may not work. But there is nothing wrong with the intention. And there need be nothing wrong with the intention to have children with a better chance of flourishing as a result of not having a disability.

But, even if the preference for normality is utterly untainted by the ugly attitudes, this may not prevent it from causing dismay to some people with disability. Deborah Kent, who is blind as a result of Leber's congenital amaurosis, regards blindness as a neutral characteristic. Her daughter Janna might have inherited the blindness. She describes her husband's rejoicing when Janna first tracked his hand with her eyes: ' "She can see!" Dick exulted. He rushed to the phone and called my parents with the news. I listened quietly to their celebrations. I don't know if anyone noticed that I had very little to say.'[49]

There is a deep conflict here, where many of us will feel the pull of the values on both sides. People should not be prevented from choosing children with more rather than less potential for flourishing. And sometimes it may be good to make such choices. But there is a possible cost to the self-esteem of people already themselves disadvantaged.

I think that, other things being equal, it is good if the incidence of disabilities is reduced by parental choices to opt for potentially more flourishing children. But we should not deny the potential cost to which the expressivist argument draws attention. And we should try to reduce that cost as far as possible.

To do this, we need to send a clear signal that we do not have the ugly attitudes to disability. It is important to show that what we care about is our children's flourishing: that this, and not shrinking from certain kinds of people, or some horrible project of cleansing the world of them, is what motivates us. To think that a particular disability makes someone's life less good is not one of the ugly attitudes. It does not mean that the person who has it is of any less value, or is less deserving of respect, than anyone else.

There are two ways in which we can show this. One is by making the comparison with other medical programmes. We want to defeat cancer, not because we lack respect for people with cancer and want to rid the world of them, but because of what cancer does to people. The existence of doctors, hospitals, and pharmaceuticals is not an insult to the sick, just a sign of the platitude that illness impairs human flourishing. And the same goes for programmes that aim to reduce the number of children born with HIV. The harm the expressivist argument points to comes through communication. And so, if we have the right attitudes, clear communication should reduce or even eliminate the harm.

The second way of reducing the harm requires us to see one of the implications of our view. We want parents to have the choice of having a child without a disability because disabilities reduce the chance of flourishing. But disability is only one way in which flourishing is impaired. Poverty, bad housing, or child abuse can do so at least as much. If we single out disability among the obstacles to flourishing, the ugly attitudes may seem to be lurking there. We have to take the other obstacles just as seriously.

35

This does not mean we should have programmes offering termination of pregnancy to parents who are poor or live in bad housing. There are better ways of dealing with those problems.

But the insistence that what we care about is not disability as a special category, but rather how much our children flourish, does have one striking implication for genetic choices. It is common to say that genetic choices are acceptable when they are to avoid a disability or disorder, but objectionably 'eugenic' if they are to enhance 'normal' functioning. The medical boundary may seem the obvious line to defend against 'designer babies'. But making some enhancements may add to flourishing as much as eliminating some disabilities. If we are not motivated by the ugly attitudes, if what we care about is really not disability but flourishing, the medical boundary may be impossible to defend.

Chapter Two

Parental Choice and what we Owe to our Children

The decision about whether or not to have a child should be taken by the person or couple themselves. Some particular applications of this belief in reproductive freedom are controversial. A few have religious objections to contraception. Many more object on religious or moral grounds to abortion. And some would restrict autonomy where it requires access to techniques of assisted reproduction. But, with the exception of these areas of controversy, the idea of reproductive autonomy is widely accepted throughout much of the world. Becoming a parent makes such a difference to a person's life. The decision, being so central to what someone wants to do with his or her life, is likely to draw on deep values. It seems an outrage if the decision whether a person has a child is taken by someone else.

This idea fits with the intuitive feeling that it is an appalling cruelty if a woman is sent to prison for a period so long that, by the time she comes out, she will be too old to have children. The prison regime should be compatible with her having children, or else some other punishment should be found. The idea of reproductive autonomy also fits with the intuition that the one-child policy in China is a fearful invasion of liberty, that this method of population control could be justified only if there were *no* more acceptable alternative to some terrible catastrophe.

Is reproductive autonomy important only for the decision about whether to have a child, or should it extend to decisions about what kind of child to have? Much of the ethical debate on the uses of genetic and other technologies concerns the scope of reproductive autonomy. Some take the autonomy of the potential parents to be the key value at stake, while those sceptical about this often take the interests of the child to be central.

I will start with the case for parental autonomy, and then look at the ways in which what we owe to our children sometimes may justifiably constrain that autonomy.

THE BOUNDARIES OF PARENTAL CHOICE

Procreative liberty

Among the values relevant to the ethics of reproductive decisions, should the liberty of the potential parents have primacy? Or are the interests of the potential child paramount? Are there more general social interests that might justify restricting the choices of potential parents?

John Robertson argues for the first view: 'Procreative liberty should enjoy presumptive primacy when conflicts about its exercise arise because control over whether one reproduces or not is central to personal identity, to dignity, and to the meaning of one's life.'[1] The reason given for procreative liberty being paramount is the importance to identity, dignity, and meaning of control over whether one reproduces or not.

But, while control over *whether one reproduces or not* has this major role in our life, there is a question about whether this is true of control over the kind of children one has. Before the 1990s, people have had only the most limited influence on this, mainly by choosing their sexual partner. This natural restriction has not been seen as impairing people's sense of their own identity or dignity, or as causing their lives to have less meaning. Perhaps choices between different kinds of children could become so universal that restrictions could come to be seen in this way. But it is certainly not obvious that choosing whether to have a boy or a girl is on a par with the decision whether to have a child or not.

The choice to have a child without disability

It has been suggested that, to the extent that selection is possible, procreative liberty should include the choice to have a child without a disorder or disability. The reason given is that for many couples the decision to procreate may depend on the ability to have a healthy child.[2] The argument seems to be that to deny a couple something that they think important enough to affect their decision to have a child is to violate their reproductive freedom. But this extension is debatable. If cars are banned in part of a city that happens to include a church, and church attendance falls as a result, has the right to freedom of worship been violated?

But, even if that argument does not quite support its strong conclusion, there are good reasons for listening to parents who want to choose a child without disability.

Probably most parents hope their child will not be born with a disability. Because of the concern people rightly have for the interests of those who are disabled, this hope is sometimes frowned on. Children need unconditional acceptance. Even if disability is not mere difference, is it not better to welcome each child, able-bodied or disabled, rather than have these preferences?

Sometimes it is suggested that a preference for a child without disability is selfish, putting the desire to avoid difficulty and complication before the child's need for unconditional acceptance.

Here, everything depends on the family context and on the kind and degree of disability. Some disabled people and their families cope brilliantly with some disabilities. Sometimes the other family members are enriched. A child who has a disability may give a lot to them and, in turn, may draw out of them things they did not know they had. But some disabilities are so devastating that no parent or family should be blamed for failing to cope, or for choosing to have a child without these problems.

Some parents have been open about the problems. Julia Hollander has written about her baby daughter. Imogen has permanent brain damage. The cause of her problem was not genetic. When she was born, the placenta peeled away early, and this destroyed her cerebral cortex. Imogen has fits, and will never walk or talk. She will need help with feeding. She will be in and out of hospital all her life. She cannot smile or make eye contact. She cannot communicate except by crying. Her expectation of life is about twenty years. Julia Hollander describes the day she was told about Imogen's brain damage and her resulting 'special needs' and 'profound learning difficulties'. She describes carrying Imogen out of the hospital, like the other mothers with babies in car seats: 'But mine was carrying a time bomb, a terrifying future ticking away. We needed help.'[3]

Julia Hollander also describes how limited any support is, and how hard it is to get. The paediatrician mentioned respite care to the community nurse, who replied: 'I don't think there is any.' The GP said it might be a couple of years before her condition and needs would be clear, and that the social services would help only if the baby was in danger. Julia Hollander claimed disability allowance. Imogen needed such intensive care that perhaps the top allowance would be paid: in 2003 just over £56 a week, which would provide eleven hours' baby-sitting. The local 'resource centre' was said to provide help for families needing respite care, but only when the child was 5, and the centre was threatened with closure. The special-needs school costs £135,000 a year, for which some parents, after years of applying, get public support. The head teacher used the phrase 'dump and run' to describe the way those parents, unable to cope, abandoned their children to the school. A social worker advised living for the moment and not thinking about the future. This was little comfort: 'But there it is, a gigantic future where, for 20 years, I must nurse this baby in a horrible cloud of non-communication.'

Early on, the social-services assessor came to make a report, at first saying it would be a month or so before there would be any response. But, sensing the situation, she arranged foster care for a weekend. Grateful for that brief relief, Julia Hollander handed Imogen over: 'In the car I weep, drowning in shame, the humiliation of not being able to look after my own child.' After the weekend, the foster-carer said: 'She's not right, is she? Poor little thing, she must be in pain. My husband can't stand the crying.'

Such a severe disability brings out how the thought that a parent is 'selfish' to hope for a child without disability can be cruel and unfair. No one should be criticized for wanting to escape the problems faced by Julia Hollander. And parenthood is a region where the boundary between self-interest and concern for the child gets hopelessly blurred.[4] Where a child has a very severe disability, much of the parental burden may be empathy for the child's own distress. Parents may have an interest in their child not having such a disability, an interest that is serious and that should not be disregarded because of misguided moral criticisms.

41

Children's interests as a constraint on choice

How important is procreative liberty relative to the interests of the child? Are there constraints posed by what people owe to their children?

Parental hopes for an able-bodied and healthy child should not be dismissed as unimportant. There are various ways of trying to realize this hope. Someone who is a carrier of a genetic disorder such as thalassaemia may select a partner who is not a carrier. Or a couple may use pre-natal diagnosis to choose a child without a disability. Or the woman may avoid smoking and stress in pregnancy. Or there is antenatal diagnosis and the choice of termination of that pregnancy, followed by another conception.

In all these cases, the parental desire for a healthy child fits with the interests of the child born as a result of the choice. The child saved from disability by a decision not to smoke in pregnancy will be glad. The healthy child who was chosen at the stage of pre-implantation diagnosis will normally be pleased to have been born. And so on.

In some of the cases, there is a possible conflict with any interests possessed by the child not selected. The fetus aborted or the embryo not implanted is thought by some to have moral claims to life. Everyone knows these claims are highly controversial, but, for those who accept them, there is a possible conflict with parental liberty. In the case of selecting a partner without thalassaemia, there is not even a candidate as a third party to consider. Admittedly, if another partner had been chosen, a different child might have been conceived and born. But we do not owe anything to unconceived potential children. When a country limits immigration, there are people in the queue whose interests are affected by being kept out. But the immigration queue model is inappropriate here. People who are kept out by restricting immigration exist. Those kept out of the world by not being conceived are non-existent.

Because the hope to have a child without disability is unproblematic from the point of view of the child who is born, procreative liberty is not in conflict here with what we owe to our children.

But other procreative choices are more controversial. Sex selection is often opposed. Some have criticized giving fertility treatment to older women. Some have criticized using pre-implantation diagnosis to select a child whose stem cells could be used to save the life of a brother or sister. The criticisms are often from the standpoint of the potential child, and the critics sometimes question the emphasis on procreative liberty. As Onora O'Neill has said:

> Reproduction is unlike both contraception and abortion, in that it aims to bring a third party—a child—into existence ... Reproductive choice is therefore not best seen on the model of the exercise of a liberty right, such as a right to freedom of expression. Ideals of individual or personal autonomy ... are unpromising starting points for thinking about reproduction.[5]

It is surely right that, even if procreative decisions are central to the lives of parents, and even if those decisions are an important aspect of self-expression, they are not *just* acts of self-expression. Even if the desire for a healthy child raises few problems, the more controversial cases support Onora O'Neill's claim that more is at stake than parental freedom. The interests of the child should set limits to what potential parents do.

The debate over the more controversial cases, however, is not usually between people who care about what we owe to our children and people who think that procreative liberty trumps everything else. More often, it reflects disagreements about what we do owe to our children.

TWO DIMENSIONS OF ETHICS

Making the world a better place and what we owe to people

People sometimes do things that make the world a better place. They create a garden or they compose a piece of music. They invent a radio that works without electricity. They give money towards a sports centre for children. They put on a performance of a play in a hospital. People's motives may not always be purely altruistic. Doing these things can bring fulfilment and perhaps reputation. But such activities do also make the world a better place.

These activities make the world better but they are not owed to anyone. No one has a right to complain if I do not make a garden or invent a new kind of radio. There may be exceptions: you employ me to invent radios, or I am a garden-designer of genius who could be accused of squandering a unique talent. But, ordinarily, there is no need to justify not undertaking these projects. There are other things that we owe to people. Sometimes what we owe them is not to act in certain ways: not to lie about them or not to harm them. Sometimes we owe them something more positive: to help them where we are in a position to do so, or to keep a promise to them.

The natural habitat of much morality (of all morality, some would say) is the region of 'what we owe to each other'. This is territory where, as Thomas Scanlon has said, we aspire to justify our decisions to others on grounds they could not reasonably reject.[6]

Which grounds others could reasonably reject often depend on who those others are. Different people can have different claims on us, sometimes because of commitments or promises made.

Often it is a matter of relationships. When claims are not met, husbands and wives, partners and lovers, parents and children, or friends, can reasonably require stronger reasons than might do for others. Without those reasons, we are open to their reproach.

Other claims, by contrast, are universal. Everyone has some claim to recognition and respect. Jeff McMahan has suggested that the aim of justifying our conduct towards others by appealing to principles that they could not reasonably reject is itself one interpretation of what it is to respect them.[7] Another basic claim that anyone can make is about harm. 'You harmed me when you could have avoided doing so. What justification did you have for that?' Another reproach is: 'You were in a position to save me from something bad. Why did you not do so?'

Future generations and impersonal harm

Derek Parfit has argued that choices affecting future generations raise a special problem. When we are choosing between different policies, the choice we make may well mean that different people are born. This is true of many economic and environmental policies and of many technological developments. (Parfit asks: 'how many of us could truly claim, "Even if railways and motor cars had never been invented, I would still have been born"?')[8] Some decisions that will probably make the world worse in a few generations (such as those that speed up climate change) will also mean that different people are alive then from those who would have been alive had we acted differently.

The people who will live if we choose the worse policy will not themselves be harmed by our choice. They will be glad to be alive, which they would not have been if we had chosen the better policy. So they cannot reproach us with failing to give *them* what we owed to them. We could say that this shows choosing the environmentally worse policy is not wrong, since no one is made worse off than he or she would have been. But this seems the argument of an over-ingenious defence lawyer. Surely we have done wrong, because we have made the world a worse place?

This seems right. But a consequence is that, in these decisions affecting future generations, morality cannot be simply a matter of what we owe to people. Some serious harms are 'impersonal', with no one being denied anything owing to them. To criticize the bad environmental policy, we have to make comparisons of the relative well-being of different groups of people. Parfit calls this the Non-Identity Problem.

The same point can be made about decisions about who is born. If parents choose to have a child with one genetic make-up rather than another, where each kind of child would flourish, but the one chosen would have less potential for flourishing than the other, any criticism of the choice has to be based on the comparison. It cannot be based on any claim about the child not getting what he or she was owed.

Our thinking about ethics has to change to accommodate this point. But there are two different ways in which it might change. One approach is supplementary. It accepts that there is an extra dimension to ethics. There is one kind of moral objection when what you do gives someone personal grounds for reproach: 'why did you do this to me?' And there is a different kind of moral objection when you do something that makes the world worse, even if no one has personal grounds for reproach.

Quite often, on the supplementary view, these two objections will both hold. It is objectionable to make the world a worse place, and it is even more objectionable when this also wrongs a particular person. If you kill a magnificent tree by pouring poison on its roots, you make the world a worse place. But if your neighbour owns the tree, your behaviour is even more objectionable.

An alternative approach treats the fact that the world has been made a worse place as the only objection to what has been done. Parfit has argued for a version of reproductive ethics in which this impersonal objection is a replacement rather than a supplement.

Should we exclude 'what we owe to people' from reproductive ethics?

Parfit appeals to a thought experiment. Suppose there are two medical programmes, each aiming to reduce the incidence of a particular inborn disability. People with the condition have lives that are still well worth living. But they still see it as a disability, something they would prefer not to have had. It can be caused by either of two medical problems in the child's mother. The first problem affects the child during pregnancy. The second problem, which always disappears in two months, affects the child if the woman has it at the time of conception.

The first medical programme targets the risk in pregnancy. It tests pregnant women for the relevant condition. Those testing positive are treated and so their children avoid the disability. The second programme targets the risk at conception. Women intending to become pregnant are tested for the relevant condition. Those who test positive are advised to postpone pregnancy for at least two months.

The pregnancy programme means that each year 1,000 children who would have had the disability are born without it. The preconception programme means that 1,000 women who would have had a child with the disability instead have a different child without it. So, in terms of reducing the incidence of the disability, they have the same outcome: there are 1,000 fewer people a year with the disability.

Suppose there is funding for only one of the programmes and so we have to decide between them. Is their moral importance equal, or does one of them have a stronger moral claim than the other? In support of their equal importance is their equal contribution to reducing the incidence of disability. But there is a possible difference between them based on what we owe to people. If we reject the pregnancy programme, there will be people who can say that we left their avoidable disability untreated. The reproach is that we owed it to them to give them the medical help they needed. While, if we reject the pre-conception programme, the resulting people with the disability are glad to have been born. The programme would have prevented their birth, so they are glad it was rejected. They cannot reproach us with failing to prevent harm to them.

Are the two programmes equally important because of their equal contribution to reducing the incidence of the disability? Or does it make a moral difference that rejection of the pregnancy programme leaves some people with the reproach against us that we did not give help we owed them?

To discuss the contrasting views, we need to compare two medical programmes with the same quality of outcome. Perhaps a disability is harder to bear if you know that people could have prevented it but chose not to do so. So, in the case of rejecting the pregnancy programme, Parfit suggests we assume that those born with the disability do not know they could have been spared it.

On this assumption, Parfit argues for the first view, that the pregnancy programme has no moral priority over the pre-conception programme. He accepts that a greater reduction in the incidence of the disability would be better. But, either way, there will be the same number of people with the disability. The difference is that one of the two groups could have been cured. He says that the fact that either group has the disability is bad.

He goes on to ask: 'Would it be *worse* if, unknown to them, their handicap could have been cured?' He accepts that it would have been morally worse if those in this group were worse off than those in the other group would have been if we had made the other choice. But the fact that, unknown to them, they could have been cured does not make the quality of their life worse. 'Since this is so, I judge these two outcomes to be morally equivalent. Given the details of the case, it seems to me irrelevant that one of the groups but not the other could have been cured.'[9]

The factors that Parfit allows to count against a decision about the programmes come from only one of the two dimensions of ethics contrasted here. Differences in the incidence of the disability, or differences in how hard it is to bear, are both relevant to whether we make the world a better or a worse place. What about the other dimension? Do people have grounds to reproach us for not providing what we owe them? This dimension is hard to notice in the case of the two medical programmes. They are made comparable by stipulating that people do not know that the pregnancy programme would have protected them. So there will be no actual reproaches. But this should not obscure the possibility that *grounds* for reproach may exist. Perhaps we do owe treatment to those who will get it under the pregnancy programme? If so, what we owe to them is not changed because they are unaware of it.

The relevance of both dimensions

The Non-Identity Problem shows that we can make the world a worse place without harming particular people, and that this matters. But we do not have to accept that this is *all* that matters.

Take choosing to have a deaf child. (To avoid a complication, assume that this is in a society in which cochlear implants have not been developed.) Potential parents can exercise their freedom to have a deaf child. The child is not harmed. There is a question I will be discussing later of whether there is a moral obligation to choose a child with maximum potential for human flourishing. Probably most people do not think there is such an obligation. Certainly it is hard to see that parents should be *forced* to choose children with maximum potential.

But, as Tony Hope and John McMillan have pointed out,[10] there is a contrast with the case of deliberately intervening (say, at the fetal stage) to make a hearing child deaf. In 'impersonal' terms, the outcome of the two choices is the same. Whether a deaf embryo is selected or a potentially hearing fetus is made deaf, the outcome is a deaf child. But, on the second choice, there will be a deaf child with the justified reproach that he or she has been harmed. There would be a justified reproach against the parents who did the harm, and one against the society that failed to protect the child by stopping them.

WHAT DO WE OWE TO OUR CHILDREN? A DECENT CHANCE OF A GOOD LIFE

Many parents (perhaps most? perhaps nearly all?) want above all what will be best for their children. So seeing what parents owe to their children as a *constraint* on their choice will often be misleading. When the relationship goes well, the emotional closeness makes a bond so strong that the interests of the parents are bound up inextricably with those of the children. As Thomas Murray has pointed out, the contrast between selfishness and altruism loses its force here.

The language of obligation is not the most attractive way of thinking about the parent–child relationship. Where things are going well, it should be unnecessary. But things do not always go well. And some ways of not being 'a good enough parent' involve not giving children what they are owed.

So what do we owe to our children? There is likely to be widespread agreement that a lot of what we owe to our children has to do with their having good lives. There is some strain in thinking of all the parental contributions to a good life in terms of what children are owed. Being loved is important, but we may hope that not too many parents have to see loving their children as an obligation. Much of what children need from parents is in this way better if it flows spontaneously. But, if a parent does not feel warmly enough to provide enough support spontaneously, food and shelter, protection and kindness, are among the minimal conditions of a good life a child is owed.

Encouraging and respecting their autonomy is also something we owe to our children. There is good reason to think the growth of autonomy is part of a good life. So it may seem unnecessary to treat it separately. But, since people's autonomous decisions sometimes impair their own lives, there may be a conflict between respecting someone's autonomy and doing what is best for him or her overall. In such a conflict there are two values at stake. So there is a case for treating autonomy separately. Here we will start with having a good life.

When our children *are* still children, they need many things if they are to have a good life. There are obvious physical needs: food and drink, shelter and warmth, clothes, and medical care. They have non-physical needs too: love and warmth, security, the chance to make friends, stimulus, being talked to and being listened to, and the chance to develop their talents and themselves. We owe these things to our children so that they can have a good life *while* they are children. But we also owe all this to them in childhood so that they can later have good lives as adults. If they are deprived of these things, their lives are severely limited. This is so even if they are glad to be alive. It is still so even if they have the contentment that comes from having adjusted to their limited lives.

In the previous chapter, I suggested that the claim that 'it is not fair on the child', often made against proposals to give help in having children to post-menopausal women or lesbian couples, is one of the most misused arguments in reproductive ethics.

I am sceptical about there being *any* disadvantage (other than having to deal with social prejudice) that comes from having a lesbian couple as parents. It is true that having a post-menopausal mother means that she is more likely to die when the child is younger, and that the child will experience her declining years earlier. But none of this comes anywhere near making life not worth living. And, when we are not misled by the adoption model, we see that the choice for that child is not between a post-menopausal mother and a younger mother, but between being born to the post-menopausal mother and not being born at all. Children with lives worth living have not been harmed by being born.

This may have created a degree of justified alarm. The message seems to be that it is fine to have a child, or to give reproductive help to someone, so long as the child's life is expected to be at the level where it is just worth living. This may seem an alarmingly low standard. A child's life has to be very terrible before people think that euthanasia might be an issue, or, at least, think that it would have been a mercy if the child had not been born. Can it be right to bring a child into the world so long as we expect the child to have a quality of life at least at the zero line just above that 'very terrible' level? Is it really acceptable to aim so low?

The answer 'yes' can be called the 'zero-line' view. Contrast this with the 'perfectionist' view that there is a moral obligation to aim for the child with greatest potential for having a good life.

Perfectionism

Perfectionism is an ethical view that a good human life consists in the flowering of certain aspects of human nature, which, as far as possible, should be cultivated.[11] In the history of philosophy, perfectionists have normally advocated self-cultivation. But the new possibilities of genetic choice have encouraged what could be called procreative perfectionism: the view that we should aim to have children who will have the best chance of a good human life.

There are various possible versions of the procreative perfectionist view. One would link it to social enforcement, with regulatory bodies banning assisted reproduction to people thought to be likely to be less good parents, or banning the use of donors likely to pass on deafness or other disabilities.

Other versions of the procreative perfectionism lean towards reproductive freedom. No outside restrictions are advocated. Potential parents themselves have an obligation to aim for children likely to have the best lives. This, in turn, admits of different interpretations. One might be that people should not have a child where, perhaps because of severe poverty or because of their own severe disability, they can provide only a relatively disadvantaged home. This seems to substitute moral criticism for legal restrictions on reproductive freedom. It still seems objectionably intrusive on a very personal decision.

The most liberal version of this view says that potential parents should aim for the child with the greatest chance of a good life that *they* can have. Julian Savulescu has argued this in the context of genetic testing. His Principle of Procreative Beneficence says that 'couples (or single reproducers) should select the child, of the possible children they could have, who is expected to have the best life, or at least as good a life as the others, based on the relevant, available information'.[12]

This liberal form of procreative perfectionism is not strictly a matter of what we owe to our children, since it suggests we choose some children rather than others. If we reject the 'immigration-queue' model of potential people, it is not owed to any potential child to be chosen. On our two dimensions of ethics, this liberal perfectionism is a matter of trying to make the world a better place. If the outlook became widely adopted, children's average potential for a good life would probably rise.

But, as Michael Parker has argued, there might also be some human costs. There is a danger of the variety of forms of the good life being overlooked in favour of some simplified version of 'the best life'. And the moral requirement to aim for a child who will have the best possible life is an open-ended one, which may place too great a burden on potential parents.[13] There is something to be said for avoiding the intrusion of too many or too stringent moral obligations into an intimate personal decision. There is a case against placing additional moral burdens on people having children, a case for simply welcoming whatever children are born. We may lose something if we substitute the mindset of quality control for the cheerful moral anarchy of the free-range approach.

A minimum level?

Procreative perfectionism, even in its liberal form, may place too much weight on the children having the best possible lives and so put too much pressure on potential parents. But does not the zero-line view err in the other direction? *Should not* potential parents be under some moral pressure, at least, to consider whether it is right to bring into the world a child whose life is, by a small margin, just worth living? And perhaps something similar may apply to those who provide assisted reproduction services? For instance, some victims of horrendous abuse as children may later still find their lives worth living and be glad to have been born. Does this mean that a couple with a persistent record of terrible child abuse should still be serious candidates for fertility treatment? Should there not be some minimum level above the zero line?

The case of child-abusers who ask for help in having more children raises another issue. Perhaps by their record they have disqualified themselves, removing any moral claim on other people to provide help. But the central moral question is not about those who run fertility clinics, but about the lives of the children they hope to have. Can the zero-line view really be adequate to deal with this request?

Many think the zero-line view sets the standard far too low. Where should the minimum level be set, and on what basis? Frances Kamm has suggested the line should be normality. She discusses a hypothetical case (introduced by Derek Parfit) of a woman who knows that, if she conceives now, her child will have a life worth living but will be mildly retarded. The woman also knows that, if she waits, she will be able to have a normal child. Frances Kamm accepts that, having a life worth living, the child with mild retardation will not be harmed by being created. But she thinks the woman will still have done wrong by not waiting. This is not just a comparative point, based on the fact that the alternative child would have a better chance of flourishing. She says 'even if she could produce no child except a mildly retarded one, it might be better for her not to produce any' and that the woman 'would do wrong to produce a defective child when she could have easily avoided it'.[14]

This account raises several questions. Is it only the predicted *medical* normality of the child that is necessary for the parent to avoid moral censure? What about someone in serious poverty having a child, whose predicted circumstances will be an equally serious obstacle to flourishing? What about a child who will be seriously disadvantaged by racist or religious hostility? If only medical disadvantage is relevant, why is that special? If other kinds of disadvantage count too, what is the level of economic or social disadvantage that should exclude people from having children, and what are the reasons for drawing it in one place rather than another? And, perhaps more fundamentally, if the child will not be harmed by being brought into the world, what is the basis on which parental choice to have the child is judged to be wrong?

Another way of drawing the line is proposed by Bonnie Steinbock and Ron McClamrock. They suggest that a decision to have children is morally acceptable only if it satisfies a 'principle of parental responsibility'. People should, where possible, refrain from having children if they cannot give them 'a decent chance of a happy life'.[15] They consider the case of creating a child whose life predictably will be 'marked by pain and severe limitations'. Could it be right to do this? They say the answer must be 'no'. The only reason for saying 'yes' could be that the child, although miserable, is not so badly off as to long for death. They say: 'That is not the kind of answer a loving parent could give.'

This is an appropriate comment on the particular case. Of course, a lot depends on what 'marked by pain' means: mild pain several times a year, or fairly serious pain most of the time? Assuming pain towards the serious end of the continuum, a decent parent would surely see this as a reason against having the child. Bonnie Steinbock and Ron McClamrock make the point that this is not only or mainly because this additional pain makes the *world* a worse place. Such an account would leave out 'the plausible and intuitive idea that bringing children into existence under very adverse conditions is unfair to the children themselves'.[16]

Yet there is a problem about the idea that in having such a child we are being unfair to that child, the idea that we owed it to such a child to prevent his or her conception or birth. The claim seems plausible enough if we focus on the pain. But it seems less plausible if we focus on the fact that, despite the pain, the child is glad to be alive. If this is really so, how can it be that we owed it to the child to prevent his or her life?

It is true, as Bonnie Steinbock and Ron McClamrock point out, that there can be cases where someone is glad to have been treated unfairly or to have been denied what he or she was owed. They cite possible cases where a victim of injustice becomes rich and famous as the result of the publicity. But the gladness in such cases is not about the injustice in itself, but comes from compensating consequences external to it. In the case of creating a child with a life including both pain and good features that the child will think enough to outweigh the pain, potential parents considering what they owe to the child need to take both sides into account. The good side of the child's' life is not some compensating factor 'external' to the injustice of creating the child, but something relevant to deciding whether it would be unjust.

The zero line and the grey area

One thing that makes discussion of these issues so difficult is that the idea of the zero line, below which life is not worth living, is largely a philosophers' abstraction. In real life, if we wonder whether a certain problematic kind of life is worth living, or is a good one, we may be overcome with the difficulty of giving an answer. Of course, there are clear cases. Some people are healthy, have warm and deep relationships, are creative in their work, and are clearly happy with the way their lives are going. At the other extreme, where a baby has died after enduring a serious disorder for several painful months, the parents may be quite clear that it would be cruel to have another child who had to go through the same thing.

But other cases may dwarf our imagination. One person may have no close friends or family, and may spend a life in and out of prison. Another may be severely demented. We may feel at a loss about whether either of them is likely to find such a life worth living, let alone how to interpret any preference they may have. In reality the 'zero line' is often hidden somewhere inside a huge grey area, where only a monster of self-confidence would come up with an easy judgement—or a judgement at all—about someone's life being above or below the line.

The phrase used by Bonnie Steinbock and Ron McClamrock, 'a decent chance of a happy life', is relevant here. It is wrong knowingly and voluntarily to bring into the world a child whose life will fall below the zero line: a life so bad that 'it would have been a mercy if he or she had not been born'. But, because of the grey area, decisions will more often be about serious risk of such a life. Parental responsibility suggests avoiding bringing into the world a child who will run a serious risk of a life not worth living. That seems roughly equivalent to saying that the child has to have a decent chance of a happy life.

This thought that we owe to our children a decent chance of a good life is intentionally vague. It is a rule-of-thumb test, which leaves a great deal to assessment of particular people and circumstances. But some plausible things can be said about certain decisions the test might rule out or allow.

Some of the controversial cases would not plausibly be ruled out by this test. It is hard to see that having an older mother, or having lesbian parents, or being born with a disability such as deafness, in themselves raise a serious risk of a life not worth living. Being a teenage mother, one of the cases Bonnie Steinbock and Ron McClamrock want to exclude, would not be ruled out on this version of the principle of parental responsibility.

But other cases would plausibly be excluded. The couple with a history of serious child abuse should not be given fertility treatment. There is no total certainty, but the risk of the child having a life not worth living is a serious one. (Ignore here the complication that, if the authorities know of the previous child abuse, the couple is unlikely to be allowed to keep the child anyway.)

Then there are disorders that, at the least, pose a serious risk of the child having a life not worth living. Take Lesch–Nyhan syndrome, a rare genetic disorder found only in males. The body produces too much uric acid. Consequences include impaired kidney function, blood in the urine, deposits of uric acid crystals in the urine and under the skin, kidney stones, muscle weakness, arthritis, painful swelling in the joints, difficulty in swallowing and eating, vomiting. It involves mental retardation and speech impairment. Associated with it are muscular spasms and involuntary writhing, as well as violent flinging of arms and legs. There is irritability and compulsive aggression (often later regretted) towards others: kicking or head-butting them, spitting or vomiting on them. There is also compulsive self-harm: head banging, biting their own lips or fingers, poking their own eyes, or putting their fingers in the wheelchair spokes. The people who have the disorder do not want to be hurt and so are afraid of the onset of the compulsion to harm themselves.

Without treatment, children with the disorder have a life expectation of less than 5 years. Treatment with allopurinol reduces the build-up of uric acid and so extends life expectation to 40 or more. But there is no treatment for the neurological condition. Attempts to contain the consequences of the compulsion to harm themselves include helmets, restraining devices, secured arm protectors and mittens, and tooth guards or the extraction of teeth.

Having never known anyone with this condition, I am reluctant to say that it is incompatible with having a life worth living. But it must carry a serious risk of a life not worth living. The test proposed here, presumably in line with the thinking of most potential parents, would urge avoidance where possible of giving birth to a child with this condition.

Genetic disability as a natural injustice?

Where someone has a disability, there is the thought that life has treated him or her unfairly. Should correction of disabilities be seen as a matter of justice?

Disadvantages have different origins, with different implications for whether or not those who have them suffer an injustice. Disadvantages caused by the avoidable actions of other people are the most obvious candidates for injustice. If pollution from your chemical plant has damaged my health, my claim against you for medical treatment and compensation is a matter of justice. Less obvious, but increasingly accepted, are the links between justice and other people's failure to act to prevent a disadvantage. It used to be thought natural or inevitable that disabled people could not use certain buildings, trains, and buses. But strong campaigning has made us see that failure to provide disabled access is a choice and that this 'passive exclusion' can also be an injustice.

Both of these kinds of disadvantage, those arising from other people's avoidable actions and from their avoidable failure to act, are candidates for injustice because of the link to someone else's responsibility. There is a contrast with 'natural' disadvantages: those outside human control. 'Natural' disadvantages are not normally seen as an injustice.

This contrast fits with widely accepted ideas about equality of opportunity. If some people are worse off because social arrangements disadvantage them (as when they are provided with less good schools) this is seen as an injustice to be corrected. Equality of opportunity is generally seen as requiring action to reduce socially caused disadvantage. But it is not usually thought to require the correction of 'natural' inequalities. Where different people have equally good schooling, and success goes to those with more ability, few think this unfair. People's different 'gifts' are seen as outside the realm of redistributive justice. To the extent that these gifts are inborn rather than the result of the social or home environment, this seems to support their exclusion from the domain of justice. The existence of inborn differences is seen as something independent of what others have done, and so no question of compensation seems to arise.

But the possibility of genetic intervention and choice makes this less simple. Allen Buchanan and his co-authors argue that, to the extent that genetic technology gives us increasing control, genetic disadvantage should come to be seen as injustice. They predict and advocate 'the colonization of the natural by the just'.[17] On this view, where genetic intervention to correct a child's disability is possible, it should be seen as part of what we owe to that child.

This seems right. We owe to our children other forms of medical treatment that they need, and gene therapy (unless it affects the child's identity) is not different in principle. The qualification needed is that in some cases the harm of the disability may need to be weighed against other things.

The reason for genetic intervention against disability is to promote the child's chances of flourishing. But flourishing can be affected by other factors, such as lack of money. We do not think that parents have to sacrifice absolutely anything in order to earn more money and so enable their children to escape from poverty. A balance may have to be struck between parental freedom and the flourishing of the children, whether that flourishing is limited by poverty or by disability. Something similar is true of other maternal–fetal conflicts of interest—for instance, where a woman does not want a Caesarian section that is in the medical interests of the child. As Rosamund Scott has argued, there is no single answer that fits all cases. A lot depends on how serious is the child's medical interest and what the woman's reasons for refusal are. A lot also depends on how the conflicting interests of the mother and of the child relate to each other.[18]

It is relevant to the Caesarian-section issue that the child is still inside the mother's womb. This would apply to any gene therapy proposed after implantation. If the disability is relatively minor, the mother may be reasonable in rejecting very invasive procedures needed for the gene therapy.

Some disabilities may be eliminated only by means that are a great burden for the parents. But, with this qualification, it seems right that there should be 'the colonization of the natural by the just'. Where an obstacle to flourishing can be eliminated in a way that is not unreasonably burdensome, its removal is something we owe to our children.

Parental freedom and the good life of the child

Parental freedom should be constrained by the interest of the child in having a good life. Where a particular child can be saved from disability by genetic intervention, this is something parents owe to the child unless there are strong countervailing reasons.

Where choosing between different possible children is in question, how far should parental freedom of choice be subject to moral constraints? I have resisted the degree of incursion that would go with the perfectionist view, that there is an obligation to choose the child that has the best chance of the best life. That approach intrudes too much moralizing into the intimate parental choice to have children. I have defended a version of the zero-line view as carrying with it a moral obligation. But the version is a cautious one, taking serious risk of falling below the line as the test. And nothing here is said against parents who want to aim for a child with the greatest chance of flourishing. I have some sympathy with them, but do not want to say their policy is morally obligatory.

WHAT DO WE OWE TO OUR CHILDREN? RESPECT FOR IDENTITY AND AUTONOMY

Playing God? Experimenting with people

Does parental choice slide into 'playing God'? The religious objection to 'playing God' is not about what we owe to our children. The charge is blasphemy, in replacing God's design with our own. But there is also a secular version of the objection: we should recognize our limitations as designers of life. The charge is one of hubris, but it is rooted in what we owe to our children.

The hubris is partly a matter of being too dismissive of risks. In the case of gene therapy, the technology may be less safe than we suppose. A disaster with this technology may do irreversible damage affecting someone's whole life.

There is also the charge of being oblivious of another kind of mistake. In human life, there is a recurring theme of overconfident

63

reconstruction. Parts of towns that have evolved over centuries have been torn down to make room for modern shopping centres and for traffic-flow schemes. Missionaries and colonial administrators have embarked on 'civilizing' missions among only partly understood 'natives'. Communists and other revolutionaries have aimed to create a new kind of human being through the radical transformation of society. Enthusiasts for capitalism have thought history can be ended by the imposed global penetration of the free market. After all these failed projects, with their human costs, can we be sure that planning the genes of our children will mean they have more flourishing lives?

Another version of the charge of hubris is independent of any blunders we may make in genetic planning. Even if our genetically designed children turn out to have wonderful lives, do we have the right to decide what they are to be like? Do we owe them a form of respect that excludes taking such decisions for them?

Cloned replicas

There is a much-discussed hypothetical scenario in which people try to overcome death by cloning themselves. Such a project would be naive. The genetically identical child is mistakenly seen as a continuation of the parent. But genes are not everything. Identical twins need not have identical personalities. And, even if they did, they would still be different people. My cloned child may be alive in eighty years' time, but I will still have died.

Someone might still think that having a cloned replica child would be the next best thing to personal survival, and so want to try cloning. Such a parent sees the child in an unattractively egocentric way. Does this show that the project would be morally objectionable?

It is likely to be a disadvantage for a child to have a parent with this attitude, but not such a disadvantage as to make being alive a matter of regret. This again raises the issue of the required minimum level of flourishing.

There is also the objection that a child created as a replica is treated, not as an end in himself or herself, but merely as a means. In one of its versions, Kant's Categorical Imperative tells us to 'treat humanity, whether in your own person or in the person of any other, never simply as a means, but always at the same time as an end'.[19]

This Kantian principle is both very important and very hard to pin down. The importance is obvious. 'I came to see that he was just using me' is a damning moral criticism. (For instance, when he married her for her money.) But there are all sorts of ways in which we quite unobjectionably 'use' each other all the time. When I catch a bus, I am 'using' the bus driver as a means to going somewhere. But, so long as he freely chose the job, and so long as I treat him with appropriate respect, there is no moral problem about this way of 'using' him. (He may be said to be, equally unobjectionably, 'using' me to earn his living.) The key phrase is 'never simply as a means'. The word 'simply' stands in for such conditions as freely choosing a job rather than being a slave, not being deceived in a relationship, and being shown appropriate recognition and respect.

So the fact that the parent is using the cloned child as a means to a version of personal survival does not settle the question of whether the Kantian principle is being violated. People quite often have mixed motives for having children. ('We hoped having children would save our marriage.' Or, 'We thought it would be nice for Fred to have a brother or sister.') Whether the child is treated merely as a means depends on how much the parents love and care for the child. If the quest for a substitute version of personal immortality leads a parent to force the child to develop in only one direction, Kantian worries are supported. But, otherwise, the criticism is weak.[20]

There is a report of a father whose child died and who wanted to create a clone of that child. He wrote a letter in which he said: 'I would never stop until I could give his DNA—his genetic make-up—a chance.'[21] In commenting on that parent's plan, Thomas H. Murray drew on his own experience of the loss of a child: 'There are no technological fixes for grief; cloning your dear dead son will not repair the jagged hole ripped out of the tapestry of your life.' He wrote of 'the fruitless quest to quench your grief in a genetic replica of the son you lost'.[22]

Thomas Murray is right about the futility of the project. Cloning will not bring back the lost child. But, if a bereaved parent goes ahead with cloning, hoping the genetic similarity will be some comfort, is this open to moral objections?

It is likely to be a disadvantage to the child to have the weight of the parents' memories of their previous child. But it is unlikely that this burden will be great enough to create a serious risk of life not being worth living. So it is more plausible to object on the grounds that the new child is being treated merely as a means. Once again, the force of this objection depends on the details of the particular case. If memories of the previous child are used to cramp the independent development of the cloned child, who is given no recognition as a distinct person, the objection is strong. But, if the parents love the new child as a new person, and welcome and encourage emerging characteristics that differ from those of the previous child, it is hard to see that the Kantian objection has force. In general, the search for a cloned replica seems pointless rather than morally wrong.

Having one child to save another

Sometimes parents of a child with a serious medical condition want to have another child whose stem cells may be used to save the life of the first child. *In vitro* fertilization, followed by pre-implantation genetic screening, was used by the parents of a young girl with Fanconi's anaemia: Molly Nash. Fanconi's anaemia is a rare genetic disorder causing bone marrow failure and other major problems, including cancers. Children with this condition reach adulthood only if they have a transplant of bone marrow or of umbilical stem cells. Molly's parents chose an embryo without the anaemia and whose tissue matched hers. (Only two of the fifteen embryos fitted these conditions.) Adam Nash was born as a result. Taking the stem cells from his umbilical cord caused him no physical harm or pain. The stem cells were used to save Molly's life.

There have other cases since. This use of pre-implantation screening has been criticized, sometimes as an objectionable form of eugenics. More often the criticism is that it treats the new child merely as a means. Lord Winston described it as 'using an unborn child as a commodity'.[23] How strong an objection is this? Is the child chosen to save another child being treated merely as a means?

As in the case of a cloned replica, everything depends on the details of the particular case, though here, unlike the rather pointless cloning of a replica, something very serious is at stake. If ethical objections had stopped the Nash parents from using pre-implantation screening, this would most likely have resulted in Molly's death. The ethical objections that could justifiably block the only means of saving a child's life have to be very impressive indeed.

For someone to be treated merely as a means, there has to be a violation of his or her autonomy or else a denial of some kind of respect he or she is owed. It is true that the placental cells are taken without the new child's consent. Obviously, the newborn baby cannot be consulted about this, just as the embryo could not be consulted about being selected for implantation. Because there is no capacity for choice, the issue of respecting the child's auto-nomy does not arise at either stage.

A lot depends again on the context and on the particular facts. Adam Nash was a wanted child. But, in the hypothetical case of parents who put their second child up for adoption after having him or her *simply* to save their first child, there would be force in the objection that the second child had been treated merely as a means. It also matters that the second child is not harmed by the use of cells from the placenta. The Kantian objection would have considerable force if parents had a second child in order to have an organ donor for the older child. This requires so much more of the second child and raises serious issues about how genuine any consent to the donation would be. But the objections to these hypothetical cases do not apply to the case of a wanted second child selected for having genes that would enable stem cells to save an older sibling. A child's life is at stake. An unobjectionable proposal should not be blocked by a blurred version of the Kantian principle that fails to distinguish between different cases.

What right had you to decide what I am like?

How far should parents, or other people bringing up children, be free to determine the children's character and identity? Is someone who belongs to a religious cult suitable as an adoptive parent, or should the children be protected from being 'brainwashed' into the values and beliefs of the cult? If the cult members are unsuit-able as adoptive parents, what about the protection of their own natural children? Should they be removed by the state? What marks off a 'cult' from any minority religion that seems eccentric, or indeed from any religion we happen not to believe in? There is a difficult boundary to draw between legitimate protection of chil-dren (for instance, when parents on their behalf refuse life-saving medical treatment or blood transfusions) and a dictatorial lack of respect for beliefs and practices we do not share.

As well as the political conflict between respect for diversity and the protection of children, there is the underlying issue about parenting. People determined that their children should be very like them are egocentric. They are quite likely to be stifling parents. But totally avoiding the shaping the beliefs and values of our children may not be desirable either. It is certainly impossible. So where do we find the mean between the extremes?

The egocentric parents who want to reproduce their own characteristics in their children are stifling because they leave no room for the children's own self-creation. Of course, people's personality and character are not just their own creation. Both biological and environmental factors set limits to what we are like. But those limits leave some scope for self-creation.

For most people, self-creation is not a heroic lifetime project. John Rawls talked of people having 'life plans'.[24] But most of us are not psychological architects on such a large scale. Our self-creation is piecemeal, not always fully intended, and not always even fully conscious. We influence our character and personality by decisions we take for other reasons: by the person we marry or live with, by the children we have, by the job we take, or by where we live. Then there is the self-creation Aristotle noticed. An action may be repeated, sometimes often enough to become a habit. And habits in turn harden into character traits.[25] Haphazard as all this often is, our role in shaping ourselves is something many of us value. Usually we do not want *other* people controlling how we develop.

Before children are old enough to decide for themselves, decisions taken for them by someone else can irrevocably damage their chances of adult autonomy. Joel Feinberg suggested that future autonomy, and some other interests, should be held in trust for people while they are too young to be in charge themselves. He called this 'the right to an open future'.[26]

Given that parents inevitably have great influence on a child's outlook and values, which in turn will shape the process of Aristotelian self-creation, how should parents give proper respect to the value of self-creation? Young children cannot consent. They cannot say how much parental influence they will accept. An alternative test asks whether, as adults, they will be glad of what their parents did. But there is the problem that the values guiding the adult person's retrospective consent have been shaped partly by those parents.

Joel Feinberg said that the best way for parents to respect self-creation is to give the child as much input as possible at every stage. Heredity and early environment will mean that even infants will be drawn in certain directions. Parents should be guided by this. And, as an increasingly formed self emerges, with its own dispositions and values, these should play an increasing role in the creation of a still more fully formed later self. A good parent increasingly steers where the child wants to go, and at the very least 'will not try to turn him upstream and make him struggle against his own deepest currents'.[27]

David Heyd makes a similar point, using the metaphor not of a river but of a tree. He proposes a 'concentric' view, in which a person's identity is formed as a tree grows, layer by layer from the core to the surface. A new branch is constrained by what has already grown. It in turn creates options for new offshoots. The central core of a person's identity is what matters, but the distinction between surface and core varies at different stages. As peripheral branches become stems and set limits to further development, the core is continually enriched and expanded.[28]

David Heyd accepts that the shaping of people's identity is only partly under their own control. The influence of the parental environment and biological factors is likely to be very deep and also hard to reverse. But he sees the question of which characteristics form our essential core as something we can each decide for ourselves. And, to the extent that self-creation is possible, we can revise our identity in ways that would be objectionable if other people tried to do so.

I agree with Feinberg and Heyd that self-creation is something to foster. What implications does this have for parental choice of a child's genetic characteristics?

Two different values are at stake: self-creation and independence. We value an open future, one that leaves us some scope to shape ourselves. We also value our independence, the fact that our nature is not just the product of decisions by others. Both self-creation and independence are only a matter of degree. The influence of our genes on the choices we make excludes total self-creation. The influence of the parenting we are given excludes both total self-creation and total independence.

Although self-creation and independence can each be only partial, many of us value having a high degree of both. The two may come into conflict. Some parental choices (genetic or environmental) may increase our abilities and so give us a more open future with greater scope for self-creation. But the role of the parental choices in itself reduces our independence.

Just as independence can conflict with an open future, so it may conflict with other things we value. Suppose my parents could have chosen genes that, while leaving my other characteristics unchanged, would have made me find the good experiences of life more intense. Do I now think it would have been good if they had done so? I do value my characteristics not being just the product of their decisions. But in this case I might trade a bit of independence for the extra richness of experience.

Jürgen Habermas alludes to the value of independence by saying that being genetically designed would transform our self-understanding. He mentions the failed history of attempts to make some parts of the human being sacred, to draw boundaries beyond which intervention is impermissible: the resistance to vaccination, to heart and brain surgery, and to organ transplants. But he suggests that opposition to genetic design may have a more secure basis. This opposition can be seen as 'the assertion of an ethical self-understanding of the species which is crucial for our capacity to see ourselves as the authors of our own life histories, and to recognize one another as autonomous persons'.[29]

There is a question as to whether knowing our genes were the result of parental choice would make us feel any less the authors of our own life history than knowing that our genes are the product of the natural lottery. In neither case did we have any say in what they are. But it is true that too much genetic intervention might make us feel ourselves mere puppets of our parents and the technology they had at their disposal. But several values are at stake and the importance of independence from parents is not an absolute. For a richer life, or for greater power to shape ourselves, some loss of independence may be a price worth paying.

Chapter Three
Human Values and Genetic Design

During the 2003 celebrations of the fiftieth anniversary of the discovery of the structure of DNA, James Watson said: 'I am against society imposing rules on individuals for how they want to use genetic knowledge. Just let people decide what they want to do.' He said that parents should decide whether or not to give birth to a child with Down syndrome, or, in future, one with enhanced genes: 'Anything—a short child, a tall child, an aggressive child . . . I'm for using genetics at the level of the individual . . . It is best to let people try and do what they think is best. I wouldn't want someone else to tell me what to do—as long as you are not hurting someone else.'[1]

The last thought is a good beginning. Most of us are in favour of autonomy. But Watson's qualification is important: 'as long as you are not hurting someone else.'

LIBERTY, DESIGNER BABIES, AND THE HARM PRINCIPLE

John Stuart Mill, defending liberty, put forward the 'harm principle'. He claimed that 'the only purpose for which power can be rightfully exercised over any member of a civilised community, against his will, is to prevent harm to others. His own good, either physical or moral, is not a sufficient warrant.'[2] This attractive principle can be borrowed from political philosophy and applied to ethics. Some people say about sexual morality that there is only one prohibition: do not hurt other people.

Applying this to reproductive ethics suggests that those who choose to have a deaf child have done nothing wrong, since the children in question have not been harmed. For those of us who think that ethics is centrally about the effects of actions on people and their lives, this approach has great appeal. Surely what is bad must be bad for someone?

Earlier, I mentioned Derek Parfit's well-known Non-Identity Problem. His argument suggests that, when policies affect future generations, an approach based entirely on whether there will be people harmed by us is inadequate.

Our environmental policies may make the world a worse place for our descendants in several generations' time. At first sight it may seem that we owe it to our descendants not to harm them in this way. But different policies will shape the world in ways that will lead to different people being born. Our policies will make our descendants worse off. But not worse off than *they* would have been: worse off than an alternative set of descendants would have been.

If our actual descendants have lives worth living, *they* will be glad we followed the bad environmental policy, as otherwise they would not have been born. And the potential people who would have been born if we had followed other policies have not been harmed either. (We reject the 'immigration-queue' model of potential people.) No one has been harmed. This suggests that there are questions, especially ones involving future generations, where the harm principle (as usually understood) seems inadequate.

I hope to avoid this complication here, while preserving the spirit of Mill's harm principle. I propose interpreting the principle so that 'harm to others' includes 'transpersonal harms': that is, where one course of action brings about a world where those who exist are worse off than would have been the different people who would have existed on the alternative course. The harm principle needs this adaptation to cope with some of the genetic choices. To avoid some very difficult further issues about whether one population size is better than another, I assume the numbers of people are the same.[3]

That harm is done is necessary if banning something is to be justified. But it may not be sufficient to justify a ban. Some kinds of harm are too trivial to ban. In other cases the harm done by the ban may outweigh the harm prevented. (And this may apply also to moral criticism. By inducing guilt, or by creating a stifling atmosphere, it too may cause more harm than it prevents.)

Crossing the medical boundary

Many people think it is justifiable to make genetic choices only if they are 'medical'. They think it acceptable to aim to have a child that is healthy or able-bodied rather than one with a disorder or disability, but not to aim at non-medical 'enhancements'. They reject 'designer babies'.

This conventional view that it is wrong to cross the 'medical' boundary is hard to defend. Sometimes disabilities arouse a special revulsion, creating a desire to cleanse the world of them. But, without this special revulsion, the case for reducing the incidence of disorders and disabilities is that they are obstacles to people having flourishing lives. And this is equally a reason for making other choices, including genetic ones, to remove non-medical impediments to flourishing. Eliminating a genetic disposition to shyness or laziness might help someone flourish, as might making them more cheerful or boosting their ability to sing or to learn languages.

One day it may come to seem that we owe some 'enhancements' to our children. Or, choosing children who have a greater potential for flourishing may come to seem a good way of making the world a better place. Those who want to defend the medical boundary need to say what is special about *medical* obstacles to flourishing. What makes them the only candidates for elimination by genetic choices?

One defence of the medical boundary makes it a purely conventional one. Perhaps a 'designer-baby' world is so bad that we must seize on any barrier that may stop us drifting into it. To assess this, we have to look at whether such a world is worse than ours, and at whether defending the medical boundary is the best way of resisting it.

The genetic supermarket, inequality and entrapment

Robert Nozick rejected regulation of genetic choices. He coined the phrase 'the genetic supermarket'.[4] Why not let parents buy the genes they choose? This idea shocks many people. Why?

In the early days of the debate on genetic enhancement, some of the objections raised (such as that it would be 'un-natural') were based mainly on emotional revulsion ('the yuk factor'). Some people still have this kind of revulsion. But one result of twenty years' discussion is that these responses have been questioned and largely put aside. Now, the serious debate is in the spirit of the harm principle and reflects concern for people. The impact of genetic enhancement on human flourishing, on the kinds of lives people will lead, is central. So is the importance of autonomy and of people's claim to equality of respect.

The general approach here will be in the spirit of the modern debate. We should restrict liberty only when something comparably important to human flourishing is at stake.

But, from this James Watson's conclusion that society should impose no rules does not just follow. *Do* current or future choices between different kinds of children really pass the test of doing no harm? We have seen that *some* of these choices (though fewer than is often thought) may be open to criticism because they are against the interests of the child.

Genetic choices may cause more diffuse kinds of harm by changing the kind of society we live in. One concern is about the implications of eugenics. Here we are assuming the rejection of any state eugenic plan. It is about genetic choices by individuals or couples. But even this 'liberal eugenics' raises concerns. Could leaving people free to choose genes for their children at the genetic supermarket have serious social costs? If so, we may need a regulated market, on a European model. On this system, there would be no state plan to change people's genes or to improve the gene pool, but there might be limitations on genetic choices thought to be against the public interest. Social intervention would act only as a filter. Which choices, if any, should be excluded would be part of democratic debate.

There is a real question about whether either a general ban on genetic enhancement, or the regulated version of the market in genes, is possible. Bans or regulation in some countries might be ineffective, just leading to genetic tourism. And we have seen how hard it is on a global scale to set limits to the market—for instance, to protect ourselves against the consequences of global warming. But the issue is so important that it seems worth working out what regulation if any is desirable, even if there is no certainty of successfully setting it up. At stake is the future composition of the human race.

What concerns might support restricting the genetic supermarket? Here I want to propose a framework, indicating values that should guide us, without attempting to assess their importance relative to each other. Some concerns are about the dangers of uniformity. Is there a danger that many people might make similar choices and so diminish human variety? Other concerns are about genetic inequalities and about possible kinds of genetic competition. Others are about the possible threat to central parts of human nature.

One issue should be mentioned, if only to be put aside. No assumption of genetic determinism is made here. We all know that genes are only part of the causal input that makes us what we are. To borrow the culinary metaphor used by Patrick Bateson and Paul Martin, they are only some of the items in the 'developmental menu', alongside all the influences brought to bear in the womb, at birth, in childhood, and beyond.[5] But, equally, no assumption of genetic irrelevance is made either. To the extent that genes have input into desired human physical or psychological characteristics, people may have reasons, even if only of a probabilistic kind, for wanting their children to have those genes. It is the implications of choices based on those reasons that we need to consider.

Suppose genes affect energy, intelligence, and a range of skills. Suppose that these qualities affect economic success. Suppose that rich people can afford to spend money on purchasing for their children genes for these qualities. We are used to the way money runs in families, partly through inheritance and partly through educational and other environmental advantages. Will genetic differences come into the loop? Is there a danger of a genetically based caste system? Some have even suggested that humans may no longer form a single species as the 'gene rich' and the 'gene poor' grow further apart.

Gene-linked inequalities may exist within a single society. Or, just as the discrepancies of wealth between rich and poor countries dwarf those within a country, so the biggest genetic differences might come to exist between advanced and developing countries. Access to genetic techniques might repeat the pattern of access to health care.

This is a prospect that repels many of us. But we sometimes accept that the value of a benefit to a minority outweighs the inequality involved. Few accept the 'dog-in-the-manger' version of egalitarianism according to which, if all cannot benefit, no one should. Private swimming pools should not be banned because not everyone can afford one. There is the possibility that benefits to those genetically enhanced could outweigh the drawbacks of inequality, especially if access was likely to spread to everyone in time.

Another question is why *genetic* inequalities are worse than others. One possible answer is that genetic inequalities go deeper than economic ones. Someone once said that the rich are different from us: they have more money. Genes are not in that way external, but may affect the core characteristics of a person. But money already buys education. It is not obvious that genes affect a person's core more than education does.

A further objection to genetic inequalities between groups is that they are particularly hard to reduce. If the price of genetic enhancement does not come down enough to allow everyone access, this problem may be acute. Once in place, genetic inequalities will be to some extent automatically replicated in future generations. Rich people can give away their money. Wealth can be taxed and educational advantage restricted. But, without an appalling degree of invasiveness, it is hard to envisage the reduction of genetic advantage.

In principle, these inegalitarian implications of a market in genes could be controlled, perhaps by banning the market altogether, or by some system of regulation. But the prospects for this may be poor. As we know, global efforts to limit or regulate the market in the interest of wider values have had very limited success.

One aspect of inequalities is competition. If genetic enhancement is available, some parents will choose it for their children. This will put pressure on other parents to do the same. 'What we owe to our children' may start to include avoiding their being disadvantaged in the genetic race. Leaving our own children to the genetic lottery while others are being given a genetic boost may come to be seen as parental acquiescence in genetic injustice.

Entering this competition may in some ways make us all worse off. The economist Fred Hirsch made the point that many things people choose are what he calls 'positional goods'. For instance, in getting a job, it may be an advantage to have a university degree. This competitive advantage is one reason why some people value going to university. As a result more people may apply and universities may be expanded to meet the extra demand. But, when more people have a degree, the competitive advantage in the job market is less. To keep ahead, it may be necessary to do a Ph.D. Then the cycle may repeat itself. And so on. Obtaining positional goods, valued only for their comparative advantage, has its own costs, as in the years of your life spent in lonely and narrow scholarship for the Ph.D. We have collectively walked into a trap. As Fred Hirsch puts it, 'if everyone stands on tiptoe, no one sees better'.[6]

The genetic competition could in this way be a trap. Assuming that there are some costs to selecting genes, whether financial or having to go through IVF and pre-implantation diagnosis, parents may all be standing on tiptoe without their children seeing any better.

But there may be some compensating advantages. Sometimes people do see better. Take the case of university education. Part of its appeal may be as a positional good. But—perhaps this is my bias as a university teacher—those who go to university for the job advantage sometimes find it does other things for them too. They find molecular biology or medieval history utterly absorbing, or philosophy pushes them to rethink their beliefs and values. Or they discover Proust, or Tolstoy. Perhaps they fall in love with the poems of George Herbert, or with one of the intelligent and beautiful fellow students around them. In the case of genetic competition, parents might choose to increase the chance of features their children would be glad to have. Even if your parents chose intelligence, energy, and creativity for really bad reasons, you may still not regret their choice.

SHOULD WE DEFEND A CENTRAL CORE OF HUMAN NATURE?

We need to explore some of the underlying values at stake in making genetic choices. So it is important not to be limited to the particular genetic choices that current technology makes possible. In the future we will understand more about the role of particular genes in people's characteristics. It is likely that we will have available more, and less heavy-handed, ways of selecting genes than we have now. As a thought experiment, suppose all technical barriers to choosing genes were swept away. Of course these thought experiments have severe limitations. But sometimes we need to stand back and ask where we are going and where we want to go. Unconstrained by current practicalities, are there ethical barriers we should not cross?

We are thinking about cases where people's genetic characteristics are the result of other people's choices. Some have said that this in itself is enough to remove the human status of both parties.

C. S. Lewis said of those who might exercise genetic choices that they are 'not men (in the old sense) at all'. He says they are 'men who have sacrificed their own share in traditional humanity in order to devote themselves to the task of deciding what "Humanity" shall henceforth mean'. And he says: 'Nor are their subjects necessarily unhappy men. They are not men at all: they are artefacts. Man's final conquest has proved to be the abolition of Man.'[7]

In speaking of people deciding what 'Humanity' shall henceforth mean, Lewis clearly had in mind some large-scale planned social programme, rather than a parental choice for a particular child. It is right to worry about state eugenic planners. Even so, more argument than he gives is needed for the claim that they have sacrificed their human status. (Could they not take their decisions in the light of human values?) It is even more implausible to deny human status to parents who choose to have a child without the gene that causes Lesch–Nyhan syndrome.

The more interesting, but morally alarming, claim is that those with a genetic make-up that has been chosen are not men or women at all, but artefacts. This is alarming, because it denies human status to any child who has had gene therapy. It denies the humanity of anyone whose parents used pre-implantation genetic diagnosis to select a hearing child or a deaf child, or a child without Lesch–Nyhan syndrome. Those who disapprove of selecting a deaf child surely are not committed to rejecting the child's human status. And the contrast between being human and being an artefact needs more support. Many of our characteristics are 'artefacts' of parental choices about our upbringing and education. Why are parental *genetic* choices so different as to negate a child's human status?

Although it is unconvincing to say that chosen genes are necessarily incompatible with being human, there is a real worry behind the inflated claim. There are some possible unintended outcomes of genetic choices that most of us would now be appalled by. Some parents might choose for their children dispositions that would tend to make them more successfully competitive. Suppose that resulted in their having a deep emotional coldness. One thought might be that in being given the chance of greater worldly success they had been denied humanity.

This in turn prompts the more general thought that there may be aspects of our present human nature that we value too much to be willing to put at risk.

One threat to these characteristics could be that parents would opt against them. This may seem paradoxical. How can 'we' value them so much if 'parents' choose not to preserve them? Surely 'we' must include parents? But parents may be acting inside the competitive trap, thinking we owe it to our own children not to leave them disadvantaged in positional goods. Despite choosing that way when we have to, we might still be glad to have the choice itself removed from everyone.

Because of genetic linkage, aspects of human nature that we value could also be threatened as an unintended result of other choices. Is there a central core of human nature that should be protected against destruction or erosion? Should some genes have preservation orders?

Francis Fukuyama has given one answer to this question: 'And what is that human essence that we might be in danger of losing? . . . From a secular perspective, it would have to do with human nature: the species-typical characteristics shared by all human beings qua human beings. That is ultimately what is at stake in the biotech revolution.' He claims that ideas of morality and human rights are rooted in human nature, so that 'the very grounding of the human moral sense' is also at stake. He takes as central the idea of human dignity: 'the idea that there is something unique about the human race that entitles every member of the species to a higher moral status than the rest of the natural world.'

What properties do humans have that confer this special status on us? Would any change to what had previously been a universal human characteristic erode moral status? It is hard to see that someone genetically engineered to have green hair should lose the claim to human dignity. The issue seems to be one of deciding which characteristics are essential to being human and which are merely contingently universal. But there are two problems with this way of seeing it.

One problem is that it is not clear how we should identify the essential characteristics of a human. Before modern reproductive technology, some might have said that being born in the womb of your genetic mother was essential. But now we do not think that children of surrogate mothers are not human. In searching for essential characteristics, we seem to be looking, not for some fact, but for a definition. And it is unclear whether there is any non-arbitrary 'right' definition, at least when we are thinking of problem cases previously not thought of, such as people with some genetically engineered features.

Another problem is that, even if we did have a way of identifying essential characteristics of human beings, some of them might be terrible. There seems no guarantee that the list would include only things like rationality and imagination and not things like cruelty and aggression. If a good argument showed that some terrible characteristic—which, by genetic means, we could change—was essential to being human, it might be better to transcend the limits of humanity rather than stay as we are. The idea of what is essential is a murky one, but, even if it were not, its importance is unclear. What is worth preserving is what is *valuable*, and the connection between the two is not obvious.

Fukuyama does not seem to think that *all* universal human characteristics have to be preserved, as he mentions some that can plausibly be seen as central: consciousness, reason, feelings, and the capacity for moral choice. But he suggests that the whole human being is greater than the sum of these central features: 'It is all of these qualities coming together in a human whole . . .'.[8]

Fukuyama's account is suggestive, but leaves unanswered questions. Why *these* characteristics? How do we decide on the boundaries of the part of human nature to be defended?

Any attempt to answer these questions is an exploration of values that we humans have. The idea of transcending the human perspective is impossible, perhaps unintelligible. (This does not mean that we have to place less value, for instance, on the suffering of members of other species. One set of human values includes the idea of animal rights.) Some of the values we have are plausible candidates for being part of the central core to be preserved. Perhaps, on reflection, we will decide that some of our present values do not have to be preserved. But, inevitably, any decision about that will be taken from within the framework of our values. There is no judging from a completely external perspective.

There are two plausible starting points for the exploration of what we value in human nature. The first is the recognition that our nature, as well as having many features we may find good, also includes dispositions that can be destructive and disastrous when unchecked. So it may be fruitful to explore the countervailing parts of our nature, the parts that may keep the destructive side in check. The second starting point is the idea of the good life for human beings.

Containing the dark side of human nature

Unsurprisingly, the case for preserving human nature emphasizes its more attractive parts. It would be tragic if we lost the parts of our psychology that are visible in acts of altruism, honesty, friendship, and love. But there is also the psychology that contributes to war, torture, tyranny, and terrorism. There may be some truth in the Manichean view that our nature is divided between the light and the dark. There is a dark side that is excited by violence and cruelty, which sees people of other tribal groups or with other beliefs as enemies. But there is also part of us that feels and hates the suffering or humiliation of others, that looks at our dark side and wants not to be like that.

One problem in appealing to our values to decide which parts of our nature should be defended is that there is so much dispute about basic values. Anyone wanting guidance about the foundations of morality will find huge disagreements among philosophers and others about the fundamental principles.

But, when we think about containing or diminishing the dark side of our nature, there is quite wide agreement at a different level. Nearly everyone is appalled by massacres, by torture, and by genocide. We may have little consensus about the fundamental ethical principles that make them so appalling, but we do not find it hard to agree that they *are* appalling. By investigating the psychology that makes them possible, we may find some parts of human nature that are *not* worth preserving. But such a claim should be made cautiously, as the same psychology that contributes to atrocities might be responsible for good things as well. Or it might be genetically linked to some valuable features.

Consider an implausibly simple and extreme scenario. Suppose the overall contribution of some characteristic turns out to be unambiguously bad. (Candidates for this might include dispositions to aggression, to uncritical obedience, tribalism, fanatical belief, and so on.) Suppose this characteristic turns out to have a genetic basis. And suppose it has no genetic links to valuable characteristics. And suppose, perhaps particularly improbably, that there is no social or educational strategy that could eliminate or modify it.

We are right to be frightened by the dangers of any state eugenic programme. Positive choices of characteristics should be left to parents, subject to some possible 'public-interest' regulation of the options available. And it is hard to see enough parents making genetic choices against a bad characteristic to eliminate it. Perhaps, instead, we should look at the countervailing parts of our psychology (such as empathy, sympathy, and imagination) and consider putting a preservation order on genes relevant to them.

Without unacceptable large-scale eugenic planning, dealing with genes relevant to our darker characteristics is likely to be a matter of containment rather than elimination. And the hope is that the simple and extreme scenario underrates the possibility of non-genetic means of containment.

The good life for human beings: two versions

To the question about what parts of human nature should be protected from being altered, one set of answers is given by the need to contain our destructive side. Another set of answers is given by thinking about what a good human life is.

We are the products of evolution. Perhaps there is no unchanging central core of human nature. If there is such a central core, we do not have to accept that all of it is worth preserving. Our capacity for destructiveness and cruelty may be just as 'central' as generosity or altruism. The question should not be about which features make up the central core of human nature, but about which ones contribute to the central core of a good human life. Which they are depends on what we think a good human life is.

In the history of philosophy there have been repeated attempts to give a clear and convincing account of a good human life. Here

I will draw on two dominant traditions. In one tradition the key concept is human flourishing. In this book disability has been contrasted with human flourishing. But the idea of human flourishing may not fully capture the good life. For the other tradition, the key concept is happiness. This has its limitations too. Both terms are used in different ways, sometimes contrasting with each other and sometimes overlapping. I will suggest that the best account of the good life comes somewhere in the overlap between some versions of human flourishing and some versions of happiness. The two traditions are not very far apart, but some of the differences between them could lead to divergent policies when confronted by genetic choices.

Human flourishing

Earlier I argued that disabilities should be understood as obstacles to flourishing, and that much of what we owe to our children has to do with their flourishing. Is there anything general that can be said about what human flourishing is? The good life for human beings is unlikely to be the same as the good life for chickens or for crocodiles. Our nature is different from theirs. Which aspects of our nature are most important for what the good life is?

A minimal, Darwinian view of human flourishing might specify only the physical and psychological functions needed for survival and reproduction. But, obviously, having these functions is compatible with having an awful life.

An alternative is the 'normal-functioning' version of human flourishing. This explains flourishing in terms of having the physical and psychological functions possessed by a 'normal' member of the species. These functions may have evolved because of their contribution to gene survival, but they are now seen as needs for different reasons. For instance, Philippa Foot says that human beings need the mental capacity for language and that they need 'powers of imagination that allow them to understand stories, to join in songs and dances—and to laugh at jokes'.[9]

Although there are questions about the boundaries of normality, this account of flourishing is useful as a contrast with disability. But it is inadequate as an account of the good life. People with disabilities can have good lives and people without disabilities can have bad ones. And the account seems too conservative. It seems to place no value on enriching people's lives in ways that take them above normality. The list of human goods tends to be drawn up on the basis of human life as we know it. There may be capacities, activities, and experiences that, being as yet untried, have not made it onto the list. We might still value them if we encountered them.

One danger of an account of this sort is that it may leave out how life feels. A life rich in the normal human capacities may still not be a flourishing life if the person takes a jaundiced or depressed view of it. The cards you are dealt make a difference, but so does how you play them.

Both the Darwinian and the normal-functioning accounts of human flourishing are too narrow. This makes it attractive to move towards an account in terms of certain 'human goods', things that contribute to what we understand a good human life to be.

Martha Nussbaum gives one account of these human goods.[10] She includes health, nourishment, shelter, sex, and mobility, as well as being able to use the senses and to imagine, think, and reason. Her account includes family and other relationships, attachments and love. Also on the list is living a life one has thought about and chosen, in one's own surroundings and context. There is also laughter, play, and living in contact with the natural world. One strength of such a list is that it gives an account of what is recognizably a good life for us rather than for Martians.

Martha Nussbaum's approach is a liberal version of Aristotelianism. It is not confined by the idea of normality. Her version takes account of how life seems to the person who lives it. And she explicitly recognizes that any list of distinctively human characteristics must be open-ended, to allow for the possibility that 'some as yet unimagined transformation in our natural options will alter the constitutive features, subtracting some and adding others'.[11]

Happiness

The main alternative to the 'human-flourishing' account of the good life is the utilitarian account in terms of happiness. This has the advantage of being based from the start on how people feel about their lives. But, notoriously, accounts of happiness given by utilitarians have sometimes been too narrow.

The simplest account of happiness is the 'experience' version. Jeremy Bentham gave this its classic expression: 'enjoyment of pleasures, security from pains'.[12] Obviously pleasure is an important part of the good life. And pain often makes life less good. But the experience version is far too narrow to capture the good life. Robert Nozick's classic 'experience-machine' thought experiment neatly makes the point. Imagine some future machine that can stimulate the brain to give any set of experiences. The machine's programming can be adapted to the tastes of the particular person. As a result, people can be offered a lifetime of experiences of intense pleasure and no pain. Would you be willing to be hooked up to such a machine for the rest of your life?

Most people asked this question say 'no'. Sometimes this is for reasons that are practically important but philosophically superficial. Can we really rely on the technology? How do we know the programmer is benevolent? Do we not need a bit of bad experience to heighten the pleasure by contrast? As this is a thought experiment, we can just postulate reliability, benevolence, and just the right small dose of bad experience needed to maximize the pleasure.

But people say 'no' also for deeper reasons, reflecting features of the good life that go beyond blissful experience. Nozick lists three of these. We want to do things, not just passively to receive experiences. We care about the kind of person we are. But someone floating in a tank has no characteristics: 'plugging into the machine is a kind of suicide'. And we also want to be in touch with a reality that is not artificially constructed by people.[13]

Over many years I have asked people their reactions to the experience machine, and have been struck by the way that even those who have not read Nozick's book often make his objections. This suggests that many people have ideas of the good life that make Bentham's experience version seem narrow.

The thought experiment is a powerful counter-example to the experience version of the good life. But it is no objection at all to a different utilitarian account. This sees happiness as the satisfaction of desires. The more people's desires are satisfied, the greater their happiness. (Though the satisfactions of stronger desires counts more.) If some of our strongest desires are to be active rather than passive, to be a certain sort of person and to be in touch with a reality that is not man-made, the experience machine will not give us happiness.

Compared to the experience account, the desire–satisfaction version allows for more aspects of the good life. But in turn it is too simple. The desires people have may be based on ignorance or on mistaken beliefs. So perhaps happiness should be seen as the satisfaction of informed desires: not the ones people actually have but those they would have if they only knew.

This still may be too narrow an account of happiness. Happiness can come from things that surprise us: things not thought of and so not desired. The account may also be too broad. The satisfaction of some informed desires may not be relevant to happiness. James Griffin gives the case of meeting someone on a train who tells me his ambitions. I form a strong, informed desire for his success, but never hear of him again. His later success satisfies my informed desire but leaves my life unchanged. On the other hand, my desires for the success of my children, are usually relevant. As Griffin says, we need to include only those informed desires that 'enter our lives' in the way this contrast brings out.[14]

There are also 'pathological' desires—for instance, those of misers or kleptomaniacs—which seem so distorted that losing them might be better for the person than satisfying them. Perhaps 'informed' desire could be stretched to exclude these cases. But the central issue seems to be the warping or distortion of the desires rather than any lack of information. Earlier we saw some difficulties in interpreting people's preferences for being deaf or blind. John Elster's idea of adaptive preferences ('sour grapes') and Amartya Sen's thoughts about the scaled-down preferences of women in some developing countries are relevant here. To accommodate this, the desire version of happiness has to be liberalized to include some kind of evaluation of the desires themselves. And this requires some judgement about how rich different kinds of life are. Happiness is not just contentment or satisfaction, but also requires a certain richness of life.

Both the versions of the good life (as human flourishing and as happiness) start off too narrow. They become more plausible as they are liberalized. The liberalizing tends towards convergence. The Aristotelian version has to take account, not just of 'functioning' seen objectively from outside, but also of how a life seems to the person living it. It also has to become open-ended, allowing for changes possibly going beyond current views of human flourishing. The utilitarian version has to bring in some evaluation of experiences or desires. And this evaluation is likely to be linked to some idea of a rich human life.

Binocular vision and two strands of the good life

Often it is not easy to assess how good a life someone is having. What the person says is obviously central, but may not give a complete picture. People claiming to be glad to be alive may not be telling us everything. They may be protecting their own self-respect, not wanting to be pitied. Even accurate and truthful reports need interpretation. There is the problem of how far the person's preferences and judgement have been shaped or distorted by the kind of life they have had. We need other sources of information too.

When we see the world in three dimensions, our visual system detects depth partly by combining information from both our eyes, and works out distances from the discrepancy between them. To see to the depths of a person, we need the equivalent of binocular vision: the person's own perspective and other perspectives for comparison.

The binocular vision we need corresponds to two strands of the good life. One strand is about the fit between what you want and value and what your life is like. Part of having a good life is being happy, in the (limited) sense of being reasonably content with how your life is going. The second strand is about how rich your life is in human goods: what relationships you have with other people, your state of health, how much you are in charge of your own life, how much scope for creativity you have, and so on.

The contrast between the two strands of the good life is clear in Aldous Huxley's *Brave New World*. (The brilliance of this book, published in 1931, was to raise issues so deep that, as the genetic choices now become possible, they are still at the core of the ethical debate. It is one of the great philosophical thought experiments.) The people in the Brave New World are totally designed and shaped by their rulers. There is no room for individual creativity. Relationships and pleasures are all shallow. Because their preferences have been deliberately shaped so that they like what they get, they are totally contented. Yet we can see how limited their lives are.

The hope of shared values

What is it to 'see' the limitations of the lives of people in the Brave New World? How are such judgements about what is or is not a good human life shaped? In thinking about these issues we have two major resources.

The first resource is the sciences relevant to the study of mankind. These include the biological sciences, from genetics and evolutionary psychology to the neurosciences and neuropsychology. They also include the social sciences: anthropology, sociology, and parts of history, economics, and psychology.

Our second resource is subjective experience, seeing human nature from the inside. This includes our own subjective experience. It also includes the cumulative record of life experienced from the inside to be found in the humanities, especially in art and in novels, plays, and poems. There are also the more subjective parts of history and psychology. And there is the history of reflection on experience to be found in philosophy, particularly the continuing discussion of the good life.

In thinking about what in human nature is important to preserve, we need to make use of both the resources. Again the metaphor of binocular vision seems right. To see in depth, we need to see our nature from both perspectives. We need the outer and the inner view: both the objective perspective of the sciences and the internal, subjective perspective. Here I assume that the contribution of the sciences to our understanding of human nature is obvious. But something needs to be said about the other, inner, perspective.

It is easier to start by thinking about the good life negatively, through the bad life. Some imaginable changes in human psychology seem like nightmares. Think of people with a deep coldness, without love or friendship, having no emotional bonding with their children. Or imagine people with no curiosity, no desire to explore and understand the world, and no inventiveness. Or suppose people with no imagination, creativity, or play: without poetry, music, sport, or humour.

In calling these scenarios nightmares, there is no escaping our own experience and the judgements based on it. The reason for saying that sight and hearing are important ingredients of flourishing came down to the value placed on them by those of us with experience of them. (Or, at least, those with experience undistorted by the destabilization sometimes caused by acquiring them late.) In the same way, judgements about the importance of love and friendship, or of curiosity and imagination, also have to depend on how those of us who know these things value them.

This may seem a flimsy and precarious basis. Is that not just subjective opinion? If someone else cares more about train spotting or stamp collecting than about emotional bonding with children, is that not just as good?

It takes all sorts to make a world. Different people flourish differently. A plausible account of flourishing is unlikely to have one blueprint. Instead there will be different ingredients variously combined in literally millions of different ways. The differences will reflect (among other things) a person's age, gender, upbringing, genes, temperament, and the influence of a particular culture and historical period.

I have a modest optimism that, underneath all this variety, there is also some degree of deeper unity. The evidence for this is suggestive but not conclusive.

Part of the evidence is that subjective judgements, particularly about what is a terrible life, often agree. There is a striking level of agreement about the reasons for saying 'no' to the kinds of life envisaged in the thought experiments of *Brave New World* and the experience machine. And, in the real world, there is the use of the same horrible punishments—for instance, solitary confinement—in different cultures and in different historical periods. This suggests at least some agreement about what people are likely to find bad. I remember once visiting a chateau in the Loire valley. In the grounds was an oubliette: a deep pit into which the person to be punished was lowered to the bottom. Each day, food and water would be lowered to him or her, but there would be nothing to do and no human contact. Sometimes people would stay there until they died, perhaps for many years. Another man and I happened to be looking down into the pit at the same time. As we looked up from it, our eyes met. Nothing was said, but for a second we shared the horror we both felt. No explanation was needed. Each of us knew that the other, as a fellow human being, felt the same.

We can also draw on the history of philosophical reflection on the good life. In the first chapter I quoted Anaxagoras's answer to the question why it is better to be born than not: 'for the sake of viewing the heavens and the whole order of the universe.' For those of us who think about and teach philosophy, it is satisfying that these sublime questions about what gives life point are now of such urgent practical importance. The history of human thought on these questions has much to contribute to our decisions. But it does not give final and conclusive answers. The debate about genetic choices continues 'the conversation of mankind' about the good life, a conversation that perhaps in principle has no end.

Neurath's boat and the Brave New World strategy

E. O. Wilson once said: 'Like everyone else, philosophers measure their personal emotional responses to various alternatives as though consulting a hidden oracle. That oracle resides deep in the emotional centres of the brain, most probably within the limbic system ...'.[15] In the context of considering genetic choices, this reminds us of the contingent and precarious basis of our values. Different genes might have given us a different limbic system, generating different 'moral intuitions' when thinking about philosophy. This raises a question as to whether philosophical investigation of our values from the inside may not be too parochial, too tied to a particular genetic inheritance, one that is contingent and alterable.

The mere fact that our values result from a contingent history, whether from a particular human history, or more generally from the evolutionary history that shaped our genes, is not enough to discredit those values. In thinking about human nature and the parts of it we should preserve, there is no standing totally outside our human values. The question, after all, is about what *we* think worth preserving.

But this does not mean that all our values are fine as they are. On reflection, we may want to modify some of them. But this comes about as the result of critical thought about them. Some things people value may turn out to be self-defeating. The Prisoner's Dilemma suggests that in some contexts this is true of individual self-interest. Perhaps more importantly, some things we value may be criticized on the basis of other things we care about. John Mackie once said to me that if human genetic engineering had been available in Victorian times, people might have designed their children to be patriotic and pious. If patriotism does not hold the place it once did, this is partly because of our experience of what the patriotic outlook can lead to, together with the value we place on avoiding the killing and misery of war.

We can abandon or modify some values and we can find ourselves acquiring new ones. But it is important that this happens because of the pull of other values. There is a parallel with Otto Neurath's thought about beliefs. He opposed philosophers who, in a Cartesian spirit, advocate a strategy of abandoning our whole system of beliefs and rebuilding it on a more secure basis. In a famous passage he made the point that we cannot abandon the whole system at once. 'We are like a sailor who, instead of taking it to pieces in dock, has to rebuild the boat on the open sea, and has to be able to build it anew out of its own best components.' Something similar is true of values. Conceivably, over a long enough time, our whole present system of values may be changed. But at any one time we have to keep enough of it afloat to support the rebuilding of the rest.

So value change should be a slow, reflective process. With genetic engineering, one short cut could be called the Brave New World strategy. Imagine a genetic change that would give people a substantial competitive advantage, but that it had the side effect of eliminating any aesthetic sense. Parents might be tempted to give their children the competitive advantage, but be worried about depriving their children of aesthetic pleasure. A supplementary genetic change might be on offer, which would make people strongly prefer not to have any aesthetic sense. Those selling the package of both changes in the genetic supermarket might say, 'With the sense of loss wiped out, there is nothing to worry about'.

As in the Brave New World, preferences and values are shaped so that people like what they get.

The contentment that results from the Brave New World strategy is not enough to win over most of us. This is because our picture of the good life goes beyond contentment. We want people to have rich lives, as well as to be contented with their lot. The value we place on this leads us to reject the Brave New World strategy. Of course, in time, we may come to criticize this value and to abandon or modify it. But, until we do that, rejecting the Brave New World strategy is part of keeping the whole process of changing ourselves under the control of human values.

THE FURTHER FUTURE

Transcending our intellectual limits?

The human race has a remarkable mixture of self-confidence and self-doubt. The self-doubt is partly about our species' chances of survival. Can we avoid destroying ourselves, either with the destructive technology of conflict we have developed or through creating some environmental catastrophe? Linked to that is self-doubt about our own nature: the psychology that may cause our destruction. The self-confidence is about our capacity to understand the world. No other species, at least on our planet, has come anywhere near our capacity for increasing our intellectual grasp of what the world is like. In two or three thousand years we have transformed our understanding and we still seem to be on an accelerating upward curve. Are there any limits to this?

A limit may be set by the capacities of the human brain. In Immanuel Kant there is the thought that our cognitive constitution may set such a limit. The categories and concepts, the kinds of thinking, that have evolved in our brain may be too limited for full understanding of the universe. This is a commonplace about any other species. We would be astonished if a horse or a dog had a brain capable of understanding quantum theory. Given the circumstances in which most of human evolution took place, it can seem astonishing that humans have brains that can produce and understand quantum theory. But such astonishing facts about our capacities may make us forget that we too as a species are likely to have our intellectual limits. Perhaps we will be lucky. Perhaps the universe will turn out to be of just the right level of complexity for us to understand it. But this would be a happy coincidence, one we cannot rely on.

We have already met and transcended our sensory limits. Our vision is not up to things very small or very distant. But we have developed electron microscopes and radio telescopes to overcome this. We have no sense that detects X-rays, so we have built machines to do so. We do not have sonar, but we have invented radar. Could our intellectual limitations be overcome in the same way, with computers (or technologies descended from them) as the intellectual equivalent of radio telescopes? We are already starting to do this. We all know how computers can deal with more information and at greater speeds than we can, and we are happy to have them extend our understanding of things in these ways.

But the Kantian thought is that the human intellect may be limited in a more profound way. Computers help where there is too much information for us, or where we are too slow. But perhaps the fundamental categories of thought available to us are too limited for the science that full understanding of the universe might require. We might then be able to design computers able to develop conceptual capacities beyond ours. But, while we might use them for purposes of prediction and control, we would not be able to share their understanding.

If we had reason to think that we were in this way pressing against our own intellectual limitations, we would have a choice. We could choose to expand human intellectual capacity, perhaps by some genetic redesign. Or we could choose to accept our limitations. If at that point we decide to transcend our limitations, those coming later may think of it as one of the best decisions in human history. It would keep going one of our central projects, that of increasing our understanding of the world. The alternative, to accept our limitations, would leave us with an understanding that was incomplete but permanently static. We may have to choose between genetic redesign and the end of science.

Optimism in principle, caution in practice

In the very long run, the potential to change ourselves may in such ways give us opportunities of great value. But, in the short run, we should remember that there are dangers too. There is a case for optimism in principle and caution in practice.

One of the disappointments of the debate about genetically modified crops is the failure to generate a satisfactory version of a principle of caution. With a new technology whose risks are relatively poorly understood, there is an obvious case for caution. But those who advocate 'the precautionary principle' usually state it in such a strong form that it excludes anything where the risks are not fully known. This would exclude virtually any new technology, and the advocates of genetically modified crops can easily dismiss it. Usually they do so in favour of simple cost–benefit analysis, without any extra caution because the technology is new and the risks uncertain.

In the debate between attaching infinite weight to unknown risks and attaching no weight to them, I want to vote 'none of the above'. My hope is that when we get on to the even more serious issue of genetically modified people, our thinking about risk will have improved to the extent at least of finding some way of being cautious about new and unknown risks without opting for total paralysis.

We need an adequate precautionary principle because it is important both that the boat keeps going and that it does not sink. I mentioned Otto Neurath's idea that revising our beliefs is like rebuilding a boat on the open sea. There is a pleasing parallel between this thought of Otto Neurath, who was once in the revolutionary Spartacist government in Munich, and the way the English conservative philosopher Michael Oakeshott portrayed his own political outlook.

In political activity, then, men sail a boundless and bottomless sea; there is neither harbour for shelter nor floor for anchorage, neither starting-place nor appointed destination. The enterprise is to keep afloat on an even keel; the sea is both friend and enemy; and the seamanship consists in using the resources of a traditional manner of behaviour in order to make a friend of every hostile occasion.[16]

I accept both the conservative thought that we need to keep the boat afloat on an even keel and the radical thought that we may also need to do some rebuilding as well. With genetic choices, the combination may be quite a challenge.

The open future

I have argued that, in two ways, it may be hard to hold the line at the medical boundary. Even if we think the medical boundary should not be crossed, the way the world is set up makes it difficult to stop people crossing it. But the difficulty of holding the line is partly theoretical: of finding convincing justifications for attaching importance to this particular line.

So perhaps the medical boundary is not the right one to defend. But, if we do cross it, we may want to set limits to the free market. Here, this means limits to the programme of liberal eugenics. These limits may be to prevent social inequalities becoming even more deeply rooted genetic inequalities, and to escape falling into the competitive trap set by the pursuit of genetic positional goods. They may sometimes be based on protecting the right of our children to an open future. And, perhaps most fundamentally of all, the limits may be needed to protect parts of human nature needed either for the containment of our dark side or else in a more positive way for the good life, parts of our nature that it would be tragic to lose.

But, as you will have noticed, my own conception of the desirable boundaries of the protected area is far from worked out. No doubt this is partly because my own thinking has not penetrated far enough. But it is also in part because the project of reflecting on our own values is an open-ended one. It has been going on at least since Socrates. It is not complete now and perhaps never will be.

We are extraordinarily lucky to be thinking at this time about the values that should guide these genetic choices: at the time they are just starting to be real. No previous generation has thought about human values and the good life with a chance of their thinking mattering so much.

But we should also be aware that the boundaries we lay down and the values behind them are unlikely to be permanent. Robert Nozick made a point about political theory that may apply even more to ethical thinking about what sorts of people there should be. He said: 'It is helpful to imagine cavemen sitting together to think up what, for all time, will be the best possible society and then setting out to institute it. Do none of the reasons that make you smile at this apply to us?'[17]

In thinking about what we owe to our children, one idea is the right to an open future. Perhaps an open future is part of what we should leave for our descendants too.

Notes

CHAPTER ONE

1. *Guardian*, 8 Apr. 2002.
2. Ibid.
3. Ibid.
4. Richard Hull, 'Defining Disability: A Philosophical Approach', *Res Publica*, 4(1998), 199–210.
5. Nora Ellen Gross, *Everyone Here Spoke Sign Language: Hereditary Deafness on Martha's Vineyard* (Cambridge, Mass.: Harvard University Press, 1985).
6. Ibid. 53.
7. Ibid. 51, 5.
8. Julian Savulescu, personal communication.
9. Hull, 'Defining Disability'.
10. World Health Organization, *World Health Organization International Classification of Functioning, Disability and Health* (Geneva: World Health Organization, 2001).
11. Susan Wendell, *The Rejected Body: Feminist Philosophical Reflections on Disability* (London: Routledge, 1996), 19–22.
12. Michael Thompson, 'The Representation of Life', in Rosalind Hursthouse, Gavin Lawrence, and Warren Quinn (eds.), *Virtues and Reasons: Philippa Foot and Moral Theory* (Oxford: Clarendon Press, 1995), 296.
13. Philippa Foot, *Natural Goodness* (Oxford: Clarendon Press, 2001), 25–44.

14. Alasdair MacIntyre, *Dependent Rational Animals: Why Human Beings Need the Virtues* (London: Duckworth, 1999), chs. 3, 5.

15. Wendell, *The Rejected Body*, 14, 22–3.

16. John Harris, 'One Principle and Three Fallacies of Disability Studies', *Journal of Medical Ethics*, 27 (2001), 383–7.

17. Anita Silvers, 'Formal Justice', in Anita Silvers, David Wasserman, and Mary B. Mahowald (eds.), *Disability, Difference, Discrimination: Perspectives on Justice in Bioethics and Public Policy* (Lanham, Md.: Bowman & Littlefield, 1998), 59–74.

18. Clare Sainsbury, *Martian in the Playground* (Bristol: Lucky Duck, 2000), 33.

19. Martin Milligan, in Bryan Magee and Martin Milligan, *On Blindness* (Oxford: Oxford University Press, 1995), 38.

20. Aristotle, *Eudemian Ethics*, 1216ª11.

21. Christopher Newell, 'Disability: A Voice in Australian Bioethics?', *New Zealand Bioethics Journal*, 4 (June 2003), 19.

22. Kay Redfield Jamison, *An Unquiet Mind: A Memoir of Moods and Madness* (London: Picador, 1997), 217–19.

23. Ibid. 17.

24. Jon Elster, *Sour Grapes: Studies in the Subversion of Rationality* (Cambridge: Cambridge University Press, 1983), 109–40.

25. Amartya Sen, 'Capability and Well-Being', in Martha Nussbaum and Amartya Sen (eds.), *The Quality of Life* (Oxford: Clarendon Press, 1993).

26. John Stuart Mill, *Utilitarianism* (London: Fontana (Collins), 1962), ch. 2.

27. John M. Hull, *Touching the Rock: An Experience of Blindness* (New York: Vintage (Random House), 1990), 204.

28. Ibid. 178.

29. Ibid. 139.

30. Ibid. 192.

31. Richard Gregory and Jean G. Wallace, 'Recovery from Early Blindness: A Case Study', in Richard Gregory, *Concepts and Mechanisms of Perception* (London: Duckworth, 1974).

32. Ibid. 111–14. This includes brief accounts of other cases where recovery of sight was followed by a psychological crisis. See also M. von Senden, *Space and Sight: The Perception of Space and Shape in the Congenitally Blind before and after Operation*, trans. P. Heath (London: Methuen, 1960); Oliver Sacks, 'To See and Not to See', in Oliver Sacks, *An Anthropologist on Mars: Seven Paradoxical Tales* (London: Picador, 1995), 102–44.

33. Mike May, *Mike's Journal*, http//www.senderogroup.com/mikejournal.htm, entry for 10 April 2001.

34. Ibid.

35. *Guardian*, 8 Apr. 2002.

36. John Harris, *Clones, Genes and Immortality* (Oxford: Oxford University Press, 1998), 109.

37. Rebecca Bennett and John Harris, 'Are There Lives not Worth Living? When is it Morally Wrong to Reproduce?', in Donna L. Dickenson (ed.), *Ethical Issues in Maternal—Fetal Medicine* (Cambridge: Cambridge University Press, 2002), 326.

38. Gunilla Preisler, *Cochlear Implants in Deaf Children: Integration of People with Disabilities* (Strasbourg: Council of Europe, 2001), 27.

39. Anne Olivier Bell (ed.), *The Diary of Virginia Woolf*, i. *1915–1919*, ed. Anne Olivier Bell (London: Hogarth Press, 1977), 13.

40. Jane Campbell, 'Choose Life', *Guardian*, 26 Aug. 2003.

41. Sheila Hale, *The Man who Lost his Language* (London: Allen Lane, 2003), 45.

42. This is quoted from the text of a talk given to students at Oxford Brookes University. Michael Mason sent it to me and gave me permission to use it in this book.

43. David Wright, *Deafness: A Personal Account* (2nd edn., London: Faber & Faber, 1990), 114.

44. Jacqueline Paschoud, letter in *Independent*, 8 Dec. 2003.

45. Jamison, *An Unquiet Mind*, 190–2.

46. Chris Gravell, Mike Boyd, Catherine Slater, Annabel Tall, Leslie Duffen, John Ridal, Sue Robson, Gill Ritchie, Rosie Hedges, Professor Sue Buckley, and 27 others: letter in *Independent*, 24 Oct. 2003.

47. Kate Saunders, letter in *Independent*, 24 Oct. 2003.

48. Mary Ann Baily, 'Why I had Amniocentesis', in Erik Parens and Adrienne Asch (eds.), *Prenatal Testing and Disability Rights* (Washington: Georgetown University Press, 2000), 68.

49. Deborah Kent, 'Somewhere a Mockingbird', in ibid. 57–63.

CHAPTER TWO

1. John A. Robertson, *Children of Choice: Freedom and the New Reproductive Technologies* (Princeton: Princeton University press, 1994), 24.

2. Ibid. 33, 152–3

3. Julia Hollander, 'Why is There No One to Help Us?', *Guardian*, 28 May 2003, G2, p. 16.

4. Tom Murray, *The Worth of a Child* (Berkeley and Los Angeles: University of California Press, 1996), 5.

5. Onora O'Neill, *Autonomy and Trust in Bioethics* (Cambridge: Cambridge University Press, 2002), 61.

6. T. M. Scanlon, *What We Owe to Each Other* (Cambridge, Mass.: Harvard University Press, 1998).

7. Jeff McMahan, *The Ethics of Killing: Problems at the Margins of Life* (Oxford: Oxford University Press, 2002), 246.

8. Derek Parfit, *Reasons and Persons* (Oxford: Oxford University Press, 1984), 361.

9. Ibid. 367–9.

10. Tony Hope and John McMillan, 'Ethical Problems before Conception', *Lancet*, 361 (2003), 9375.

11. Thomas Hurka, *Perfectionism* (Oxford: Oxford University Press, 1993).

12. Julian Savulescu, 'Procreative Beneficence: Why We Should Select the Best Children', *Bioethics*, 15/5–6 (2001), 413–26.

13. Michael Parker, 'The Welfare of the Child', *Human Fertility*, forthcoming.

14. F. M. Kamm, *Creation and Abortion: A Study in Moral and Legal Philosophy* (Oxford: Oxford University Press, 1992), 124–7.

15. Bonnie Steinbock and Ron McClamrock, 'When is Birth Unfair to the Child?', *Hastings Center Report*, 24 (Nov.–Dec. 1994), 17–18.

16. Ibid. 19.

17. Allen Buchanan, Dan W. Brock, Norman Daniels, and Daniel Wikler, *From Chance to Choice: Genetics and Justice* (Cambridge: Cambridge University Press, 2000), ch. 3, pp. 61–103.

18. Rosamund Scott, *Rights, Duties and the Body: Law and Ethics of the Maternal–Fetal Conflict* (Oxford and Portland, Oreg.: Hart Publishing, 2002).

19. Immanuel Kant, *Groundwork of the Metaphysic of Morals*, trans. H. J. Paton (New York: Harper & Row, 1964), 96.

20. Hilary Putnam, 'Cloning People', in Justine Burley (ed.), *The Genetic Revolution and Human Rights* (Oxford: Oxford University Press, 1999), 1–13; John Harris, *On Cloning* (London: Routledge, 2004), 34–47.

21. Brigitte Boisellier, evidence given at a Congressional hearing, quoted in Thomas H. Murray, 'Even if it Worked, Cloning Wouldn't Bring her Back', in Bonnie Steinbock, John D. Arras, and Alex John London (eds.), *Ethical Issues in Modern Medicine* (6th edn., Boston: McGraw Hill, 2003), 665–8.

22. Murray, 'Even if it Worked', 667.

23. Lord Winston, quoted in Robert J. Boyle and Julian Savulescu, 'Ethics of Using Preimplantation Genetic Diagnosis to Select a Stem Cell Donor for an Existing Person', *British Medical Journal*, 323 (2001), 1240–3.

24. John Rawls, *A Theory of Justice* (Cambridge, Mass.: Harvard University Press, 1971).

25. Aristotle, *Nicomachean Ethics*, 1114.

26. Joel Feinberg, 'The Child's Right to an Open Future', in Feinberg, *Freedom and Fulfillment, Philosophical Essays* (Princeton: Princeton University Press, 1992), 76–97.

27. Ibid. 96–97.

28. David Heyd, *Genethics: Moral Issues in the Creation of People* (Berkeley and Los Angeles: University of California Press, 1992), ch. 6, pp. 160–90.

29. Jürgen Habermas, *The Future of Human Nature*, trans. Hella Beister and Max Pensky (Cambridge: Polity Press, 2003), ch. 2, p. 25.

Notes

CHAPTER THREE

1. 'DNA Pioneer Urges Gene Free-for-All', *Guardian*, 9 April 2003.

2. John Stuart Mill, *On Liberty* (London: Fontana (Collins), 1962), ch. 1.

3. For discussion of the problems raised by different population sizes, see Derek Parfit, *Reasons and Persons* (Oxford: Clarendon Press, 1984), chs. 17–19, pp. 381–441.

4. Robert Nozick, *Anarchy, State and Utopia* (Oxford: Blackwell, 1974), 315.

5. Patrick Bateson and Paul Martin, *Design for a Life: How Behaviour Develops* (London: Vintage (Jonathan Cape), 1999).

6. Fred Hirsch, *Social Limits to Growth* (London: Routledge & Kegan Paul, 1977), 5.

7. C. S. Lewis, *The Abolition of Man* (London: Collins, 1978), 39–40.

8. Francis Fukuyama, *Our Posthuman Future: Consequences of the Biotechnology Revolution* (London: Profile Books, 2002), 101–2, 105–28, 160, 171.

9. Philippa Foot, *Natural Goodness* (Oxford: Clarendon Press, 2001), 43.

10. Martha Nussbaum, 'Aristotelian Social Democracy', in Gillian Brock (ed.), *Necessary Goods: Our Responsibilities to Meet Others' Needs* (Lanham, Md.: Rowman & Littlefield, 1998), 135–56.

11. Ibid. 146.

12. Jeremy Bentham, *The Principles of Morals and Legislation* (New York: Hafner, 1948), ch. 7.

13. Nozick, *Anarchy, State and Utopia*, 42–5.

14. James Griffin, *Well-Being: Its Meaning, Measurement and Importance* (Oxford: Clarendon Press, 1986), 16–26.

15. E. O. Wilson, *On Human Nature* (Cambridge, Mass.: Harvard University Press, 1978), 6.

16. Michael Oakeshott, 'Political Education', in Oakeshott, *Rationalism in Politics and Other Essays* (London: Methuen, 1962), 127.

17. Nozick, *Anarchy, State and Utopia*, 313–14.

Afterword

This book grew out of my Uehiro Lectures at Oxford in 2004. The lectures were a pleasure to give. Part of the pleasure came from the lively and questioning audience. Part of it had to do with the support given to practical ethics in Oxford by the Uehiro Foundation on Ethics and Education.

Tetsuhiko Uehiro set up the Practical Ethics Association as a direct result of his being a victim of the atomic bomb dropped on Hiroshima. In hospital, nearly dying of radiation sickness, he began to think about whether people could live in a way that would make future wars less likely. The Practical Ethics Association has nearly four million members in Japan, committed to avoiding hatred and conflict. Every day, thousands of them get up before dawn to discuss ethics and to think about how to further Tetsuhiko Uehiro's peaceful ideals. Sometimes, victims of atrocities want revenge. It is inspiring that Tetsuhiko Uehiro's thoughts turned in such a different direction. I am proud to be associated through these lectures with what he started.

It also gives pleasure that Mr Eiji Uehiro and the Uehiro Foundation have chosen Oxford as a base for setting up the Centre for Practical Ethics and for this associated lecture series. This can be seen as recognition of Oxford's contribution to practical ethics. This has sometimes been eclipsed by more numerous Oxford contributions to other parts of philosophy. The Oxford Faculty of Philosophy is one of the largest and most influential philosophy departments in the world. It is well known that its members at different times have made distinguished contributions to metaphysics, epistemology, philosophy of language, philosophy of mind, philosophy of history, and to the more abstract parts of ethics. Oxford also contributed to the emergence of practical ethics.

There is a widespread view that, among philosophers in the Anglophone world, concern with practical ethics started in the United States, partly with the work of John Rawls on justice and partly as the result of American philosophers' participation in debates about the Vietnam War and about abortion. It is worth adding a footnote to this story. Much applied philosophy did indeed emerge in the United States in the turbulent time of the late 1960s and early 1970s. But in Britain too, and particularly in Oxford, there was also an upsurge of interest in the application of philosophy to practical moral issues.

One manifestation of this was a seminar series on practical ethics, given for several years from 1968 by James Griffin, Derek Parfit, and me. We were perhaps rather self-consciously radical, thinking of our class as taking philosophy where it had not been before. We gave the first series the title 'Death, Misery and Morality'. We hoped that on the lecture list, among the items on Parmenides and on logical form, our series would stand out as different.

We set out to challenge the conventional wisdom, sometimes of philosophers and sometimes of people in general. James Griffin challenged the view that moral conflicts are insoluble because some values are incommensurable. He also strongly criticized the then popular 'negative utilitarianism'. Derek Parfit started his deep questioning of the moral basis of population policy, and also first expounded his Non-Identity Problem for all policies affecting future generations. I challenged the idea of the sanctity of life, and the moral significance of the distinction between killing and letting die, as well as arguing there is a much stronger moral claim on us to give money to famine relief than conventional views suppose.

It was wonderfully stimulating to debate issues new to ethics with James Griffin and Derek Parfit. But perhaps the best thing was provided by Oxford's ability to attract so many high-powered philosophy graduate students. Our vigorously participating students at different times included John Harris, Peter Singer, David Heyd, and a considerable number of others who were also to shape the field of applied ethics. In writing this book, I have been struck by how many times the people whose ideas I comment on were at that seminar.

I would not want to give the impression that the generation of philosophers in Oxford before ours had no interest in real world ethical questions. There is the view that the Oxford moral philosophers of the 1950s and early 1960s were concerned only with moral language and with such issues as whether we can derive an 'ought' from an 'is'. But this is too simple.

Philippa Foot at that time wrote on abortion and on euthanasia. R.M. Hare wrote widely on medical ethics and on other moral problems. Stuart Hampshire and Bernard Williams both wrote imaginatively and powerfully on moral issues in politics. Alasdair MacIntyre (my undergraduate moral philosophy tutor) produced stimulating books and lectures on life, the universe, and politics, at that time from a Marxist perspective. Elizabeth Anscombe wrote, sometimes dogmatically, on life and death issues and on sexual morality. Her attack on the decision to use the atomic bomb (published in the politically complacent days of the 1950s) is one of the finest pieces of applied ethics ever written. Peter Strawson from time to time said he ranked ethics low among philosophical subjects. Then, as a kind of sideshow to his work in metaphysics and philosophy of language, he teasingly wrote two utterly brilliant articles on ethics.

But, perhaps most of all, the seriousness and clarity of the work of Herbert Hart was an inspiration. His work on the moral basis of legal punishment showed how clear thinking about principles could provide a framework for a more humane penal policy. His criticisms of the doctrine of 'the enforcement of morality' were a superb piece of philosophical analysis. They also helped to change the climate of opinion that allowed gay men to be sent to prison because of their sex lives. Herbert Hart showed how philosophy could help create a freer society.

I gave these lectures aware both of the example of these distinguished predecessors and of Tetsuhiko Uehiro's hopes for what ethics could do to make a better world. This was daunting, and inevitably the lectures in various ways will have fallen short. But I hope that this awareness has made them a bit better than they would otherwise have been.

For me there was a personal reason for pleasure in lecturing on the ethics of genetic choices. Twenty years before the lectures, I had published a book, *What Sort of People Should There Be?*, on ways of thinking about the moral choices likely to be raised by genetics and the neurosciences. The differences between then and now are striking.

In this present book, I have been able to draw on much sophisticated discussion of genetic choices, as well as on social attempts to regulate the use of genetic technology as it has become available. Then, no philosophers had written on genetic issues and it was widely believed that choosing genes for children was either impossible or at least not even on the horizon. So I had to make it all up myself. The scenarios were a series of thought experiments rather than real cases. And I had to make up not only my own arguments but also most of the views I argued against. I also had to try to persuade people that some of the scenarios might become possible and so the questions were worth considering.

Another striking difference between then and now is the way people who have genetic disorders now contribute to the debates on the acceptability of genetic selection. This is a huge advance and makes my old book look thin and abstract by comparison.

Looking back at that old book, I am struck by the contrast between the genetic parts and the neuroscience parts. So many of the genetic choices have become real, while hardly any of the neuroscience ones have done so. I still think the neuroscience issues are worth thinking about, partly for their interest and partly because one day they may become real, as the genetic ones have done. But for this book the genetic choices provide enough questions.

I dedicate this book to my son David. This is not just because we are linked by genes. It also reflects my admiration for the distinctive voice of his television programmes on genetic issues. He made two films for a series on the fiftieth anniversary of the discovery of the structure of DNA. One was an account of the discovery, and another explored the ethical issues. A little of what makes him so cheering to be with is reflected in the subtlety and perceptiveness about people, and the humour, in those films. So, even if parental praise is a bit embarrassing, I hope he will accept the dedication of this book as a sign of admiration and love.

Acknowledgments

I am grateful to the Uehiro Foundation for inviting me to give their first series of Oxford Lectures, and to Julian Savulescu for proposing my name to them. Thanks also to the lively, critical, and friendly audience for many helpful comments in the discussions after the lectures. Thanks to Peter Momtchiloff at Oxford University Press for commissioning the book and for his helpfulness and tolerance in dealing with me about it. Thanks to Julian Savulescu (again) and to another reviewer for Oxford University Press for some very helpful comments on the first draft of the book.

I owe thanks to Richard Hull, whose graduate thesis on disability issues first made me realize what deep philosophical questions the concept of disability raises.

Michael Mason, a week before he died, gave me permission to quote from his powerful discussion of things he had learnt from his own experience of a stroke. Since we were at school together half a century ago, I have been stimulated by his intelligence, by his distinctive way of seeing things, and by his honesty. He probably had little idea how much his often sharp comments influenced me.

I am grateful to Rosamund Scott for discussions; her book on maternal–fetal conflict seems a model of how to write about ethical problems of this kind. On the topics of this book, I have learnt a lot from all the works I have cited and from too many others to mention. I have also learnt from conversations with Jennifer Bostock, Tony Hope, Monique Jonas, Michael Parker,

Clare Sainsbury, Elizabeth Sloss, and Dana Wensley, and again from too many others to mention. Collective mention must be made of two other groups. Those who work at the Centre of Medical Law and Ethics have put up with my foibles and have given me many thoughts about these issues. Despite great diversity of views on particular issues, they have made me feel part of a shared enterprise of bringing humane values to bear on them. The students who have done the MA in Medical Ethics and Law at the Centre while I have been there have between them a remarkable breadth of medical and other experience, which they have shared with each other and with me in lively discussions. I have liked them a lot, and have learnt much more from them than they realize.

Index

Index